INTERNATIONALER DESIGNPREIS
BADEN-WÜRTTEMBERG
UND MIA SEEGER PREIS 2021

BADEN-WÜRTTEMBERG
INTERNATIONAL DESIGN AWARD
AND MIA SEEGER PRIZE 2021

↗
DESIGN CENTER
BADEN-WÜRTTEMBERG

avedition

FOCUS OPEN 2021

DIE DIGITALE ERWEITERUNG DES FOCUS OPEN JAHRBUCHS 2021

In den digitalen Raum gelangen mit ayscan: Unter www.ayscan.de die App herunterladen oder den unten stehenden QR-Tag nutzen, den Anweisungen folgen und die mit Symbol versehenen Seiten um Bild, Film und Ton erweitern. Viel Spaß!

THE DIGITAL ENHANCEMENT FOR THE FOCUS OPEN 2021 YEARBOOK

Enter digital space with ayscan: download the app at www.ayscan.de, or use the qr-tag, follow the instructions and scan pages marked with the symbol to enjoy additional photos, films and sounds. Have fun!

Hier die App herunterladen / Use this qr-Tag to load the app

Nach diesem Icon Ausschau halten / watch out for this icon

INHALT

VORWORTE 4–11
Strategische Daueraufgabe
→ Dr. Nicole Hoffmeister-Kraut MdL 4

Design-Benchmarks setzen!
→ Wolfgang Reimer und Christiane Nicolaus 6

Let's congratulate!
30 Jahre Internationaler Designpreis
Baden-Württemberg 12

DIE JURY
Sybs Bauer 196
Sven von Boetticher 172
Susanne Ewert 110
Tina Kammer 68
Gerrit Terstiege 44
Tilo Wüsthoff 150

AUSGEZEICHNETE PRODUKTE 16–219
1 Investitionsgüter, Werkzeuge 16
2 Healthcare 46
4 Küche, Haushalt, Tischkultur 62
5 Interior 70
6 Lifestyle, Accessoires 88
7 Licht 112
9 Freizeit, Sport, Spielen 128
11 Public Design, Urban Design 152
12 Mobility 174
13 Service Design 198
14 Materials + Surfaces 206

INTERVIEWS
Domenico Farina, AMF 22
Jens Krzywinski, TU Dresden 42
Stefan Lippert, UP Designstudio 52, 204
Anne Wonsyld,
   Löwenstein Medical Technology 58
Julian Gerblinger, Panoorama Designbüro 94
Matthias Stotz, Uhrenfabrik Junghans 100
Dietrich F. Brennenstuhl, Nimbus Group 118
Mario Zeppetzauer, Formquadrat 134
Marcus Wallmeyer, Supernova Design 140
Kurt Ranger, Ranger Design 158
Ilja Klobertanz und Lionel Linke, Defortec 180
Andreas Hess, White ID 186
Katharina Schäfer, Rökona Textilwerk 212

MIA SEEGER PREIS 2021 220–237

APPENDIX A–Z 238
Adressen 239
Namensregister 242
Das Design Center
→ Let's Thank … 244
→ Alle Formate und Services 246
Impressum 248

CONTENTS

FOREWORDS 4–11
A permanent strategic mission
→ Dr. Nicole Hoffmeister-Kraut MdL 5

Setting design benchmarks!
→ Wolfgang Reimer and Christiane Nicolaus 9

Let's congratulate!
30 Years of the Baden-Württemberg
International Design Award 12

THE JURY
Sybs Bauer 196
Sven von Boetticher 172
Susanne Ewert 110
Tina Kammer 68
Gerrit Terstiege 44
Tilo Wüsthoff 150

THE AWARD-WINNING PRODUCTS 16–219
1 Capital goods, tools 16
2 Healthcare 46
4 Kitchen, household, table 62
5 Interiors 70
6 Lifestyle, accessories 88
7 Lighting 112
9 Leisure, sports, play 128
11 Public design, urban design 152
12 Mobility 174
13 Service design 198
14 Materials + surfaces 206

INTERVIEWS
Domenico Farina, AMF 22
Jens Krzywinski, TU Dresden 42
Stefan Lippert, UP Designstudio 52, 204
Anne Wonsyld,
   Löwenstein Medical Technology 58
Julian Gerblinger, Panoorama Designbüro 94
Matthias Stotz, Uhrenfabrik Junghans 100
Dietrich F. Brennenstuhl, Nimbus Group 118
Mario Zeppetzauer, Formquadrat 134
Marcus Wallmeyer, Supernova Design 140
Kurt Ranger, Ranger Design 158
Ilja Klobertanz and Lionel Linke, Defortec 180
Andreas Hess, White ID 186
Katharina Schäfer, Rökona Textilwerk GmbH 212

MIA SEEGER PRIZE 2021 220–237

APPENDIX A–Z 238
Addresses 239
Index of names 242
The Design Center
→ Let's thank … 244
→ All formats and services 246
Publishing details 248

STRATEGISCHE DAUERAUFGABE

DR. NICOLE HOFFMEISTER-KRAUT MDL

Sehr geehrte Damen und Herren,
liebe Preisträgerinnen und Preisträger,

die Designwirtschaft generierte 2019 in Baden-Württemberg einen Gesamtumsatz von 2,7 Mrd. Euro. Infolge der Corona-Pandemie ging der Umsatz der Designwirtschaft 2020 hier im Land um circa 11 Prozent zurück. Von den wirtschaftlichen Auswirkungen der Pandemie sind vor allem selbstständige Designerinnen und Designer betroffen, da vielerorts Marketingbudgets gekürzt und Kommunikationsprojekte reduziert oder ganz abgesagt wurden.

Wie die Beteiligung am Focus Open 2021, dem Internationalen Designpreis des Landes Baden-Württemberg, wieder sehr eindrucksvoll zeigt, ist die Branche äußerst vielseitig und innovativ. Dieses Jahrbuch ist daher auch ein Beleg für die Stärke und Widerstandskraft der Designwirtschaft – trotz der Pandemie.

Erfolg bei einem internationalen Wettbewerb wie dem Focus Open zu haben, ist eine hohe Auszeichnung, denn die Preisträgerinnen und Preisträger haben sich einer weltweiten Konkurrenz gestellt. Daher möchte ich Ihnen meinen herzlichen Glückwunsch zur Prämierung bei den Wettbewerben Focus Meta, Focus Gold, Focus Silver oder Focus Special Mention aussprechen!

Viele der in diesem Jahrbuch präsentierten Unternehmen und Designagenturen nehmen seit vielen Jahren teil. Im Laufe der Jahre hat sich unser Staatspreis für Design zu einem wertvollen Instrument der Wirtschaftsförderung in und für Baden-Württemberg entwickelt. Auch der diesjährige Wettbewerb hat wieder gezeigt: Erfolgreich sind die Unternehmen, die Designleistung als eine strategische Daueraufgabe im Unternehmen sehen und als wichtigen Treiber für Innovation einsetzen.

Gerade in Baden-Württemberg befruchten sich Industrie, Forschung und Designwirtschaft seit vielen Jahren gegenseitig und tragen somit kontinuierlich zur Stärkung unseres Wirtschaftsstandortes Baden-Württemberg bei. Wie diese Kooperationen funktionieren und wie auf dieser Basis neue Produkte entstehen, sind in der Regel streng gehütete Geheimnisse.

Es freut mich daher ganz besonders, dass die Leserinnen und Leser dieses Jahrbuchs hinter die Kulissen schauen können. So geben uns alle mit Focus Meta und Focus Gold ausgezeichneten Hersteller in sehr aussagekräftigen Interviews spannende Einblicke in ihre Arbeit. Wir können dadurch die Anstrengungen ein- und wertschätzen, die unternommen wurden, um die hier dargestellten innovativen Designleistungen umzusetzen.

Die Interviewpartnerinnen und -partner berichten nicht nur von der Entstehung ihrer Innovationen, sondern auch darüber, welchen konkreten Mehrwert sie durch die Investition in Designleistung erzielen. Und sie alle sind sich einig: Design steigert nicht nur den Wiedererkennungswert einer Marke oder eines Produktes. Design macht auch den Qualitäts- und Innovationsanspruch eines Unternehmens am Markt sichtbar und trägt damit nachhaltig zur Stärkung einer Marke bei. Neben den gestalterischen Fähigkeiten sind Mut und Kompetenz von Unternehmerinnen und Unternehmern wichtige Erfolgsfaktoren.

Designerinnen und Designer sind daher Impulsgeber sowie Innovationstreiber und unterstützen Unternehmen im weltweiten Wettbewerb. Ein herzliches Dankeschön gilt daher allen Interviewpartnerinnen und -partnern, die uns an ihrem Know-how teilhaben lassen!

Der Focus Open feiert in diesem Jahr sein dreißigjähriges Jubiläum. Auch dazu herzlichen Glückwunsch! 30 Jahre Focus Open sind 30 Jahre unermüdlicher Einsatz. Mein besonderer Dank und meine Anerkennung gilt den Mitarbeiterinnen und Mitarbeitern des Design Center Baden-Württemberg, die sich seit Jahrzehnten erfolgreich für den Wettbewerbsfaktor Design einsetzen.

Im Namen der Landesregierung von Baden-Württemberg wünsche ich weiterhin viel Erfolg und Mut zu neuen Perspektiven, innovativen Produkten sowie kreativen und nachhaltigen Designlösungen, die Freude machen und Mensch und Umwelt Nutzen bringen.

DR. NICOLE HOFFMEISTER-KRAUT MDL
Ministerin für Wirtschaft, Arbeit und Tourismus
des Landes Baden-Württemberg

A PERMANENT STRATEGIC MISSION

DR. NICOLE HOFFMEISTER-KRAUT MDL

Dear Reader,
dear prize winners,

In 2019, the design sector generated total turnover of €2.7 billion in Baden-Württemberg. In 2020, as a result of the corona pandemic, its turnover here in our state dropped by approx. 11 percent. First and foremost, the economic impact of the pandemic is affecting self-employed designers because, in many places, marketing budgets have been cut and communication projects either scaled down or cancelled completely.

However, as the response to Focus Open 2021, the Baden-Württemberg International Design Award, once again so impressively demonstrates, the industry is extremely versatile and innovative. This yearbook is therefore also proof of the design sector's strength and resilience – despite the pandemic.

Being successful in an international competition like Focus Open is a high accolade indeed, because the award winners have contended against entrants from all over the world. I would therefore like to offer my warmest congratulations on your Focus Meta, Focus Gold, Focus Silver or Focus Special Mention awards!

Many of the companies and design agencies presented in this yearbook have been taking part for many years. As time has passed, our state design award has become a valuable economic development tool in and for Baden-Württemberg.

Once again, this year's competition showed that companies are successful when they see design as a permanent strategic mission and deploy it as an important innovation driver.

Particularly in Baden-Württemberg, industry, research and the design sector have been cross-pollinating one another for many years, thereby continuously contributing to the strengthening of Baden-Württemberg as a business location. As a rule, how these cooperations work and serve as a basis for the development of new products is a closely guarded secret.

That is why I am particularly delighted that this yearbook gives readers the opportunity to take a look behind the scenes. In extremely informative interviews, all the manufacturers who received Focus Meta and Focus Gold awards provide some intriguing insights into their work, enabling us to understand and appreciate the efforts that were undertaken in order to implement the innovative designs documented on these pages.

Besides talking about how their innovations came about, the interviewees also explain the concrete added value they achieve as a result of their investment in design. And there's one thing they all agree on: design doesn't just increase recognition of a brand or product, it also makes a company's standard of quality and innovation visible in the marketplace, thereby helping to strengthen a brand in the long term. In addition to design expertise, courage and competence are also important success factors for entrepreneurs.

Designers are therefore both a source of fresh impetus and innovation drivers, and support companies in the face of global competition. I would therefore like to say a sincere thank you to all the interviewees who shared their expertise with us!

Focus Open is celebrating its 30th anniversary this year. Congratulations on a wonderful achievement! 30 years of Focus Open means 30 years of tireless commitment. My special thanks and appreciation for the staff of the Design Center Baden-Württemberg, who have been successfully championing design as a competitive factor for decades.

On behalf of the state government of Baden-Württemberg, I wish you every success for the future and the courage to embrace new perspectives, innovative products and creative, sustainable design solutions that not only give pleasure but benefit both people and the environment.

DR. NICOLE HOFFMEISTER-KRAUT MDL
Baden-Württemberg State Minister of Economic Affairs, Labour and Tourism

FOCUS OPEN 2021

DESIGN-BENCHMARKS SETZEN!

30 JAHRE FOCUS OPEN – 30 JAHRE AUSGEZEICHNETES DESIGN

Jedes Projekt braucht eine Initialzündung – und jemanden, der eine Vision hat und weiß, wie man diese vorantreibt. Beispiele dafür finden sich auch im diesjährigen Jahrbuch wieder in beachtlicher Zahl. Auch der Focus Open brauchte seinerzeit eine solche Initialzündung: Vor 30 Jahren kam sie von Lothar Späth, der von 1978 bis 1991 Ministerpräsident des Landes Baden-Württemberg war. »Anlässlich des Textil-Wettbewerbs hatte der Herr Ministerpräsident den Gedanken eines Designpreises des Landes Baden-Württemberg entwickelt.« Dieses Zitat entstammt der Kabinettsvorlage des baden-württembergischen Ministeriums für Wirtschaft, Mittelstand und Technologie vom 15. Februar 1988 – und es markiert einen Neustart in Sachen Designpreis. Denn Auszeichnungen für gutes Design waren nicht prinzipiell neu: Seit vielen Jahrzehnten organisierte das damalige Design Center Stuttgart die »Deutsche Auswahl« und nahm Produkte deutscher Unternehmen unter die Lupe. Ab 1987 wurde daraus die »Design-Auswahl«, die auch ausländische Hersteller einlud, allerdings nur mit Dingen, die in der damaligen Bundesrepublik Deutschland (und West-Berlin) zu haben waren. Der Ansatz Lothar Späths ging nochmals weit darüber hinaus.

DIE WELT IM BLICK

In einer Zeit, in der Internet und globale Vernetzung noch keineswegs Alltag waren, hatte Lothar Späth die Vision, die Welt mit ihren Produktinnovationen nach Stuttgart zu holen – natürlich auch mit dem Hintergedanken, der Welt zu zeigen, was Baden-Württemberg in Sachen Innovationskompetenz zu bieten hat. Der Ball wurde weitergespielt, konkrete Ziele für einen Design-Staatspreis des Landes formuliert. Schließlich teilte das Wirtschaftsministerium am 13. November 1989 dem Landesgewerbeamt Baden-Württemberg, in dem das Design Center bis 2005 verankert war, mit:

»Das Wirtschaftsministerium ist mit den übermittelten Vorstellungen zu Organisation und Gestaltung des Internationalen Designpreises einverstanden. Nach Ziel und Inhalt richtet sich der Preis in erster Linie an Industrie, Handel und Designer. Er ist Teil der Wirtschaftspolitik des Landes. Demgemäß sollen Konsum- und Investitionsgüter hinsichtlich Technik, Funktionalität, Ergonomie und Form- und Farbgebung richtungsweisend sein, wobei die Umweltgerechtigkeit hinzuzufügen ist. Dies sollte in Gesprächen mit möglichen Juroren deutlich herausgestellt werden, damit eine zu starke Ausrichtung an einem Merkmal, z.B. Ästhetik, von Anfang an vermieden wird.«

DAS NOMINIERUNGSPRINZIP

Um möglichst breite internationale Aufmerksamkeit zu erzielen, bediente man sich eines klugen Schachzugs. Nationale und internationale Größen aus Design, Architektur und Unternehmertum wurden gebeten, aus ihrem Kulturkreis diejenigen Produktinnovationen zu nominieren, die ihrer Meinung nach würdig waren, beim Internationalen Designpreis des Landes Baden-Württemberg ausgezeichnet zu werden.

Die Namensliste der ersten Jury liest sich dann auch wie das Who's who der damaligen internationalen Designcommunity. Mit dabei waren:

Lenka Bajželj, Kunsthistorikerin aus Jugoslawien und lange Zeit Generalsekretärin der Biennale für Industriedesign in Ljubljana

Robert Blaich, Designer aus den USA und den Niederlanden, tätig für Herman Miller Inc., danach Leiter des Philips Designstudios in Eindhoven

Adélia L. Borges, Journalistin aus Brasilien und Chefredakteurin von »Design & Interiores«

Achille Castiglioni, Architekt und Designlegende aus Italien

Niels Diffrient, Designer aus den USA und Pionier im Bereich Human Factors Engineering

Kenji Ekuan, Designer aus Japan, Gründer und langjähriger Präsident des Design Studios GK Industrial Associates

Hartmut Esslinger, Gründer und langjähriger Geschäftsführer von frog design

Klaus J. Maack, langjähriger Geschäftsführer und Innovationsmotor von Erco Leuchten

Stuart Wrede, Architekt und Künstler aus Finnland und den USA, u.a. von 1988 bis 1992 Direktor des Bereichs Architektur & Design des MoMA New York

Aus den Nominierungen dieser Expertinnen und Experten gingen im ersten Jahr 1991 fünf preisgekrönte Produkte hervor:

Dental-Röntgengerät »Orthophos«
Hersteller: Siemens AG; Design: Siemens Design / Edwin Wahl / Tilman Phleps

Lernspielzeug »The Voyager«
Hersteller: Texas Instruments; Design: Inhouse

Tisch »Quadrio«
Hersteller: UP&UP S.R.L.; Design: Andrea Branzi

Videokamera »CCD-TR75«
Hersteller: Sony Corp.; Design: Kaoru Sumita

Mobiltelefon »Micro T.A.C.«
Hersteller: Motorola Inc.; Design: Leon Soren / Albert Nagele / Rudolph Kropp

WOLFGANG REIMER
Präsident Regierungspräsidium Stuttgart

CHRISTIANE NICOLAUS
Direktorin Design Center Baden-Württemberg

DESIGN BLEIBT EIN DYNAMISCHES THEMA
Seitdem ist viel Zeit vergangen. Der Designbegriff ist inzwischen in aller Munde. Auch in bislang eher designfern denkenden Unternehmen und Branchen hat sich herumgesprochen, dass Design viel bewegen kann. Darum geht es jedoch nicht erst seit 30 Jahren! Bereits die legendäre »Deutsche Auswahl« hatte ein klares, profan erscheinendes Ziel: die Förderung der Wirtschaft.

Da Design heute seinen festen Platz in den Entwicklungsprozessen hat, könnte man nun sagen, die Mission sei erfüllt. Das aber greift zu kurz, denn Design ist kein statisches Instrument. Es verändert sich, wie auch die Produkte, Systeme, Services und Technologien sich wandeln. Design wird spezieller, Designerinnen und Designer dringen tiefer in die Konzepte vor und bringen ihre Innovationsexpertise immer früher ein. Damit unterliegt auch dieses Berufsbild einem ständigen Wandel. Design, könnte man sagen, wird komplexer. Genau diese Veränderungen begleitet das Design Center, sensibilisiert dafür und vermittelt Know-how, Ansprechpartnerinnen und -partner, zeigt Lösungen. Zum Beispiel mit dem Focus Open, der neben dem Status quo immer auch darauf hindeutet, was künftig wichtig wird. Das zeigt etwa der Blick in die Kategorie Materials+Surfaces. Dort wurde ein Textil ausgezeichnet, das Verbundmaterialien ersetzt und bei gleichen Eigenschaften als Monomaterial sehr viel besser zu recyceln ist. Der Hersteller? Natürlich aus Baden-Württemberg!

Design ist Impulsgeber und Innovationstreiber, das steht fest. Innovationen werden aber immer in interdisziplinären Teams vorangetrieben und verwirklicht, das bestätigen auch unsere diesjährigen Interviewpartnerinnen und -partner einmal mehr. Zur Designkompetenz gehört eben auch die Fähigkeit, sich auf Augenhöhe mit all jenen Disziplinen auszutauschen, die am Entwicklungsprozess maßgeblich beteiligt sind. Mehr noch: »Bei interdisziplinären Fragestellungen sind wir Designer dank unserer großen Schnittstellen-Kompetenzen ideale Innovationspartner«, so Professor Jens Krzywinski im Interview zum breit aufgestellten Feldroboter-Projekt, das mit der Auszeichnung Focus Meta belohnt wurde. Dieses Beispiel zeigt, dass starke Ideen umsetzbar sind, wenn die interdisziplinäre Kooperation funktioniert. Das war schon immer so und wird immer so sein – dieser Aspekt unterliegt nicht dem Wandel.

DIE NÄCHSTE GENERATION STARTET DURCH
Und wenn wir schon bei der Zukunft sind: Werfen Sie doch auch einen Blick auf den Design-Nachwuchs. Denn parallel zum Focus Open zeichnet die Mia Seeger Stiftung Abschluss- und Semesterarbeiten von Studierenden aus, die sich der sozialen Wirkmacht des Designs annehmen. Und darunter sind, das dürfen wir so sagen, Konzeptionen mit enormem Potenzial. Wir würden uns wünschen, dass das eine oder andere Konzept nicht nur Idee bleibt, sondern Wirklichkeit wird. Sie finden die prämierten Arbeiten wie immer im Sonderteil des Jahrbuchs – und natürlich auch in der Ausstellung.

VIELEN DANK!
Nun gibt es bei Wettbewerben nicht nur Gewinnerinnen und Gewinner, auch wenn lediglich diese hier im Jahrbuch aufscheinen. Viele Einreichungen haben keine Auszeichnung erhalten, die Gründe sind vielfältig und liegen in den Händen der unabhängig bewertenden Fachjury. Doch lassen Sie uns an dieser Stelle auch diesen Einreichenden sagen: Vielen Dank für Ihre Teilnahme! Und zugleich möchten wir appellieren: Bleiben Sie dran! Betrachten Sie die Nicht-Auszeichnung als Ansporn, als Optimierungsimpuls. Wagen Sie einen neuen Anlauf im nächsten Jahr – mit neuen Ideen und neuem Schwung. Sie können viel gewinnen und nur wenig verlieren – der Focus Open schont Ihre Etats, weil die Einreichungsgebühren bewusst gering sind. Damit können auch kleinere Unternehmen und Start-Ups problemlos teilnehmen: Der Focus Open ist somit auch ein Förderpreis. Eine Auszeichnung mit dem Focus Open hat sich schon für so manches neue Unternehmen als Booster erwiesen.

Danken möchten wir natürlich auch sehr herzlich unseren diesjährigen Jury-Mitgliedern, die bereits im Vorfeld der Jury-Tage viel Flexibilität gezeigt haben. Denn bis kurz vorher war unklar, ob die Produkte vor Ort oder nur per Online-Meeting bewertet werden können. Alle haben mehrere Terminoptionen freigeschaufelt. Danke auch für die vielschichtigen, konstruktiven und lebendigen Gespräche rund um die eingereichten, sehr unterschiedlichen Designlösungen. Alle Einreichungen wurden gründlich »unter die Lupe genommen« und ausführlich diskutiert!

HERZLICHEN GLÜCKWUNSCH!
Wir beglückwünschen die diesjährigen Preisträgerinnen und Preisträger zu ihren Auszeichnungen. Wir wünschen ihnen für ihre innovativen Produkt- und Konzeptlösungen viel Erfolg sowie weiterhin wertvolle und erfolgreiche Kooperationen – deren Ergebnisse hoffentlich wieder den Weg zum Focus Open finden werden. Dann mit neuer Jury, aber der gewohnten Neutralität, Seriosität und Offenheit, die den Internationalen Designpreis Baden-Württemberg auszeichnen.

KATEGORIEN

1 INVESTITIONSGÜTER, WERKZEUGE
2 HEALTHCARE
4 KÜCHE, HAUSHALT, TISCHKULTUR
5 INTERIOR
6 LIFESTYLE, ACCESSOIRES
7 LICHT
9 FREIZEIT, SPORT, SPIELEN
11 PUBLIC DESIGN, URBAN DESIGN
12 MOBILITY
13 SERVICE DESIGN
14 MATERIALS + SURFACES

KRITERIEN

✓ GESTALTUNGSQUALITÄT
✓ FUNKTIONALITÄT
✓ INNOVATIONSHÖHE
✓ ERGONOMIE
✓ INTERFACE DESIGN / CONNECTIVITY
✓ USABILITY
✓ NACHHALTIGKEIT
✓ ÄSTHETIK
✓ BRANDING
✓ ENTWICKLUNGSVORSPRUNG
✓ USER JOURNEY
✓ DIGITALE INTELLIGENZ

FOCUS OPEN 2021

49 PREISTRÄGER
13 GOLD-AWARDS
15 SILVER-AWARDS
20 SPECIAL MENTION AWARDS
1 META AWARD

DIE JURY

✓ DR.-ING. SYBS BAUER MA (RCA)
✓ SVEN VON BOETTICHER
✓ SUSANNE EWERT
✓ TINA KAMMER
✓ GERRIT TERSTIEGE
✓ TILO WÜSTHOFF

FOCUS OPEN 2021

SETTING DESIGN BENCHMARKS!

30 YEARS OF FOCUS OPEN – 30 YEARS OF AWARD-WINNING DESIGN

Every project needs an initial spark – and somebody who has a vision and knows how to press ahead with it. Once again, this yearbook presents examples of such cases in considerable numbers. In fact, Focus Open itself was born of just such an initial spark: 30 years ago it came from Lothar Späth, who was Minister-President of Baden-Württemberg from 1978 until 1991. »The textile competition prompted the Minister-President to develop the idea of a design award presented by the State of Baden-Württemberg.« This quote is taken from the cabinet bill presented by Baden-Württemberg's Ministry of Commerce, SMEs and Technology on 15 February 1988 – and marks a new start in terms of design awards. Because in principle, accolades for good design were not new: for many decades, what was then the Design Center Stuttgart had been organising the Deutsche Auswahl (German Selection) and putting products by German companies under the microscope. From 1987 on it became the Design-Auswahl (Design Selection) and was open to foreign manufacturers as well, although they could only enter things that were available in the Federal Republic of Germany (and West Berlin) at the time. Lothar Späth's approach went far beyond that.

THE WORLD IN VIEW

At a time when the internet and global interconnectedness were still far from everyday, Lothar Späth had the vision of inviting the world to come to Stuttgart with its product innovations – in part, of course, with the ulterior motive of showing the world what Baden-Württemberg itself has to offer in the way of innovation expertise. The idea was taken further, and concrete goals were framed for the creation of a state design award. Eventually, on 13 November 1989, the Ministry of Economic Affairs informed the Baden-Württemberg Office for the Promotion of Trade and Industry, which the Design Center was incorporated in until 2005, that:

»The Ministry of Economic Affairs agrees to the proposals regarding the organisation and constitution of the International Design Award. In terms of its objective and content, the award is primarily aimed at industry, commerce and designers. It is part of the state's economic policy. Accordingly, consumer and capital goods should point the way ahead in terms of technology, functionality, ergonomics, form and use of colour, as well as in terms of environmental responsibility. This should be clearly emphasised in talks with potential jurors in order to avoid too strong a focus on any particular aspect, e.g. aesthetics, right from the start.«

THE NOMINATION PRINCIPLE

A clever move was implemented so as to generate broad-based international attention for the award. Prominent national and international figures from design, architecture and enterprise were asked to nominate product innovations from their cultural environment that they considered worthy of receiving the Baden-Württemberg International Design Award.

As a result, the first jury lineup reads like a who's who of the international design community at the time. The members were:

Lenka Bajželj, art historian from Yugoslavia and long-serving General Secretary of the Biennial of Industrial Design in Ljubljana

Robert Blaich, designer from the USA and the Netherlands, worked for Herman Miller Inc., subsequently head of the Philips design studio in Eindhoven

Adélia L. Borges, journalist from Brazil and editor-in-chief of Design & Interiores

Achille Castiglioni, architect and design legend from Italy

Niels Diffrient, designer from the USA and pioneer in the field of human factors engineering

Kenji Ekuan, designer from Japan, founder and long-serving president of design studio GK Industrial Associates

Hartmut Esslinger, founder and long-serving CEO of frog design

Klaus J. Maack, long-serving CEO and innovation engine of Erco Leuchten

Stuart Wrede, architect and artist from Finland and the USA, director of the Department of Architecture & Design at MoMA New York from 1988 until 1992

In 1991, the first year of the award, these experts' nominations resulted in five prize-winning products:

Orthophos – dental x-ray machine
Manufacturer: Siemens AG; design: Siemens Design / Edwin Wahl / Tilman Phleps

The Voyager – educational toy
Manufacturer: Texas Instruments; design: in-house

Quadrio – table
Manufacturer: UP&UP S.R.L.; design: Andrea Branzi

CCD-TR75 – video camera
Manufacturer: Sony Corp.; design: Kaoru Sumita

Micro T.A.C – mobile telephone
Manufacturer: Motorola Inc.; design: Leon Soren / Albert Nagele / Rudolph Krolopp

WOLFGANG REIMER
President District Government
Stuttgart

CHRISTIANE NICOLAUS
Head of Design Center
Baden-Württemberg

DESIGN REMAINS A DYNAMIC TOPIC
A lot of time has passed since then. Meanwhile, design is on everyone's lips. Even in companies and industries that hadn't previously given much thought to the topic, word has spread that design can make a big difference. But that's been the case for a lot longer than 30 years! The legendary Deutsche Auswahl already had a clear, seemingly mundane goal back in its day: to promote economic development.

In view of the fact that design now has a permanent place in development processes, it might be tempting to say »mission accomplished«. But that doesn't tell the whole story, because design is not a static tool. It changes, just as products, systems, services and technologies change. Design is becoming more specialised, designers are more deeply involved with concepts and contributing their innovation expertise at an increasingly early stage. As a result, the profession is subject to constant change as well. Design, you could say, is becoming more complex. Those are precisely the changes that the Design Center accompanies; it raises awareness, shares know-how, puts people in touch with one another and points to solutions. With Focus Open, for instance, which not only presents the status quo but always indicates what will be important in future too. That is very much in evidence in the Materials+Surfaces category, for instance, where an award has been presented to a textile that replaces composite materials: it has the same properties, but is very much easier to recycle because it's a mono-material. The manufacturer? From Baden-Württemberg of course!

One thing is certain: design is a source of fresh impetus and an innovation driver. But innovations are always perfected and implemented in interdisciplinary teams, as is once again confirmed by this year's interviewees. Because design competence also includes the ability to exchange views and ideas on an equal footing with all the disciplines who are instrumental to the development process. And what's more, says Professor Jens Krzywinski in an interview about the broad-based field robot project that won the Focus Meta award, »When it comes to interdisciplinary questions, we designers make ideal innovation partners thanks to our considerable interfacing skills.« This example demonstrates that strong ideas are practicable when the cooperation between disciplines works. That has always been the case and always will be – that's one aspect that does not change.

THE NEXT GENERATION IS SET TO GO
And speaking of the future: be sure to take a look at the young designers featured in this yearbook too. Every year, parallel to Focus Open, the Mia Seeger Foundation presents its prize to final projects and coursework in which students embrace design's power to have an impact on society. And if we may say so, there are some concepts with huge potential among the winners. We would be delighted to see one or the other of them go beyond the idea stage and become reality. As always, the prize-winning works are presented in a special section of the yearbook – and in the exhibition too, of course.

THANK YOU!
Competitions don't only have winners, even if they are the only participants who appear in this yearbook. Many entries did not receive an award or distinction; the reasons are many and varied, and entirely in the hands of the independent jury of experts. But we would like to take this opportunity to acknowledge those entrants too: thank you for taking part! And don't be discouraged! See the non-award as an incentive, as impetus for optimisation. Try again next year – with new ideas and new momentum. There's a lot to win and very little to lose – Focus Open is budget-friendly because the entry fees are deliberately kept low. That means even smaller companies and startups can easily take part: Focus Open is thus a newcomer award too, and has boosted the fortunes of many a new company over the years.

We would also like to say a heartfelt thank you to the members of this year's jury, in particular for the flexibility they showed in the run-up to the judging. Because until shortly beforehand, it wasn't clear whether they would be able to assess the products in person or only online, and they were all kind enough to keep several dates free for us. And a big thank you for the complex, constructive and lively discussions about the very wide-ranging entries too. Every one of them was »put under the microscope« and discussed in depth!

CONGRATULATIONS!
Our congratulations to this year's winners on their well-deserved awards. We wish them great success with their innovative products and concepts and hope they continue to benefit from worthwhile and productive collaborations. We would be delighted to see the results in future editions of the Focus Open competition – which will be held with a new jury, but with the same neutrality, integrity and open-mindedness that have always been the hallmarks of the Baden-Württemberg International Design Award.

CATEGORIES

1 CAPITAL GOODS, TOOLS
2 HEALTHCARE
4 KITCHEN, HOUSEHOLD, TABLE
5 INTERIORS
6 LIFESTYLE, ACCESSORIES
7 LIGHTING
9 LEISURE, SPORTS, PLAY
11 PUBLIC DESIGN, URBAN DESIGN
12 MOBILITY
13 SERVICE DESIGN
14 MATERIALS + SURFACES

CRITERIA

- ✓ DESIGN QUALITY
- ✓ FUNCTIONALITY
- ✓ INNOVATIVENESS
- ✓ ERGONOMICS
- ✓ INTERFACE DESIGN / CONNECTIVITY
- ✓ USABILITY
- ✓ SUSTAINABILITY
- ✓ AESTHETICS
- ✓ BRANDING
- ✓ STEP CHANGE IN DEVELOPMENT
- ✓ USER JOURNEY
- ✓ DIGITAL INTELLIGENCE

FOCUS OPEN 2021

49 PRIZE WINNERS
13 GOLD AWARDS
15 SILVER AWARDS
20 SPECIAL MENTION AWARDS
1 META AWARD

THE JURY

- ✓ DR.-ING. SYBS BAUER MA (RCA)
- ✓ SVEN VON BOETTICHER
- ✓ SUSANNE EWERT
- ✓ TINA KAMMER
- ✓ GERRIT TERSTIEGE
- ✓ TILO WÜSTHOFF

30 JAHRE INTERNATIONALER DESIGNPREIS BADEN-WÜRTTEMBERG
30 YEARS OF THE BADEN-WÜRTTEMBERG INTERNATIONAL DESIGN AWARD

30!

Von Lothar Späth, dem damaligen Ministerpräsidenten des Landes Baden-Württemberg 1991 initiiert, ist der heute als Focus Open bekannte Designpreis einer der renommiertesten deutschen Awards mit internationaler Ausrichtung. In den drei Jahrzehnten seines Bestehens wurde der Internationale Designpreis Baden-Württemberg zu einer festen Größe in der Designbranche – mit ganz eigenen Qualitäten.

Initiated by the then Minister-President of Baden-Württemberg Lothar Späth in 1991, the design award now known as Focus Open is one of the most renowned design competitions with an international orientation in Germany. In the three decades of its existence, the Baden-Württemberg International Design Award has become a constant in the design sector – with its own very special qualities.

»Als ehemaliges Jurymitglied schätze ich besonders die nichtkommerzielle Ausrichtung des Focus Open. Die Jury ist unabhängig und setzt sich jedes Jahr wieder neu aus Menschen mit Designexpertise zusammen. Der Focus Open wird damit gerade von unserem Team als echte Auszeichnung erlebt.«
→ Birte Jürgensen, Director zweigrad Design in Hamburg

»Der Focus Open Design Award hat sich in den letzten 30 Jahren immer wieder neue Themen gesetzt und sich so für uns zu einem der bedeutendsten Awards in der Designwelt entwickelt. Er wird so seinem Namen gerecht, offen für die Herausforderungen der kommenden Jahrzehnte zu sein.«
→ Andreas Enslin, Leiter Design Miele & Cie. KG in Gütersloh

»Es ist der Fokus auf das Wesentliche, auf das menschliche Wohlbefinden, der Innovation in einer reizüberfluteten Welt Halt verleiht – beim Focus Open ist der Name Programm.«
→ Andreas Diefenbach, Managing Partner Phoenix Design in Stuttgart

»Focus Open – klein, aber fein! Die wichtigste Designförderung mit langer Tradition macht Spaß und motiviert! Go, Stuttgart, go. Happy Birthday!«
→ Reinhard Renner, Gesellschafter Teams Design in Esslingen

»Dass im Land der Tüftler und Denker der Designanspruch mit einem eigenen Preis wertgeschätzt wird, ist bemerkenswert. Und das seit 30 Jahren. Herzlichen Glückwunsch!«
→ Christoph Schlegel, Geschäftsführer Georg Schlegel GmbH & Co. KG in Dürmentingen

»Wir schätzen beim Focus Open insbesondere die ausführliche Produkt- und Designanalyse sowie die daraus resultierenden aussagekräftigen Bewertungen. Das zeigt uns, dass wir auf dem richtigen Weg sind.«
→ Thomas Müller, Produktmanager Alber GmbH in Albstadt

»Unkommerziell, unkompliziert und unabhängig – dafür aber engagiert und persönlich. Beim Focus Open spürt man den Idealismus und den gestalterischen Anspruch – jenseits von kommerziellen Motiven. Damit ist er für mich einer der ehrlichsten Designpreise. Beim Focus Open stehen tatsächlich noch der Mensch und das Design im Fokus.«
→ Klaus Botta, Inhaber Botta Design in Königstein/Taunus

»As a former juror, I really appreciate Focus Open's non-commercial orientation. The jury is independent and there's a new lineup every year, always made up of people with design expertise. That's why our team in particular sees Focus Open as a genuine accolade.«
→ Birte Jürgensen, director of zweigrad Design in Hamburg

»In the last 30 years, the Focus Open design award has consistently addressed new topics. As a result, we see it as one of the most meaningful awards in the design world. It lives up to its name because it's open for the challenges of coming decades.«
→ Andreas Enslin, chief designer at Miele & Cie. KG in Gütersloh

»It's the focus on what really matters, on human wellbeing, that gives substance to innovation in a world suffering from sensory overload – with Focus Open, the name says it all.«
→ Andreas Diefenbach, managing partner at Phoenix Design in Stuttgart

»Focus Open – small but special! The most important longstanding award for promoting design is great fun and motivates people! Go, Stuttgart, go. Happy Birthday!«
→ Reinhard Renner, shareholder at Teams Design in Esslingen

»It's remarkable that, in the land of inventors and thinkers, design is held in such high regard that it has its own award – and has had for 30 years. Congratulations!«
→ Christoph Schlegel, managing director at Georg Schlegel GmbH & Co. KG in Dürmentingen

»What we particularly appreciate about Focus Open is the in-depth product and design analysis and the meaningful evaluations that result from it. That shows us that we're on the right track.«
→ Thomas Müller, product manager at Alber GmbH in Albstadt

»Non-commercial, straightforward and independent – but committed and personal. With Focus Open, you sense the idealism and the creative aspiration behind it – above and beyond commercial motives. For me, that makes it one of the most honest design awards there is. With Focus Open, the focus really is still on the people and the design.«
→ Klaus Botta, owner of Botta Design in Königstein/Taunus

→ **TINA KAMMER**
InteriorPark.,
Stuttgart

SEITE/PAGE
68

← **GERRIT TERSTIEGE**
Freiburg

SEITE/PAGE
44

→ **SUSANNE EWERT**
Zielform Londonberlin,
Berlin

SEITE/PAGE
110

1 → SEITE / PAGE
   18–23

2 → SEITE / PAGE
   24, 30

3 → SEITE / PAGE
   25, 31

4 → SEITE / PAGE
   26, 32

5 → SEITE / PAGE
   27, 33

6 → SEITE / PAGE
   28, 34

7 → SEITE / PAGE
   29, 35

8 → SEITE / PAGE
   38–43

INVESTITIONSGÜTER, WERKZEUGE
CAPITAL GOODS, TOOLS

GOLD:
1. 1650
   Andreas Maier GmbH & Co. KG
   Fellbach

SILVER:
2. STIFTSCHLÜSSEL
   Wiha Werkzeuge GmbH
   Schonach

3. TAILORED BLANK LINE
   Dieffenbacher GmbH
   Eppingen

4. SMARTSOLUTIONS
   Hahn Automation GmbH
   Rheinböllen

5. TUS / DN 100
   Goldcard Smart Group Co. Ltd.
   Hangzhou
   China

SPECIAL MENTION:
6. PROBOXX
   Georg Schlegel GmbH & Co. KG
   Dürmentingen

7. BIG INK XL
   Pica-Marker GmbH
   Kirchehrenbach

META:
TECHNOLOGIE-UMSETZUNG:
8. FELDSCHWARM FSE II
   Feldschwarm Konsortium
   Dresden

Funktionalität und Design ergänzen sich ideal – das beweisen ganz klar Maschinen oder Tools für den professionellen Nutzer. Industriedesign widmet sich heute selbst speziellsten Arbeitsgeräten, strukturiert Bedienabläufe, optimiert die Ergonomie, treibt Innovationen voran und verbessert im Idealfall sogar die ökologische Bilanz. Nicht zu vergessen: Das Design differenziert die Produkte am Markt und stärkt die Marke.

Functionality and design can complement each other in ideal fashion – as is vividly demonstrated by machines or tools for professional users. Nowadays industrial design applies itself to even the most specialised equipment, structures operating procedures, optimises ergonomics, drives innovations and, at its best, even improves the ecological footprint. Last but by no means least, design also ensures differentiation on the market and strengthens the brand.

GOLD 1650 GREIFSYSTEM
GRIPPER SYSTEM

1650

GREIF-
SYSTEM

INVESTITIONSGÜTER, WERKZEUGE
CAPITAL GOODS, TOOLS

FOCUS GOLD

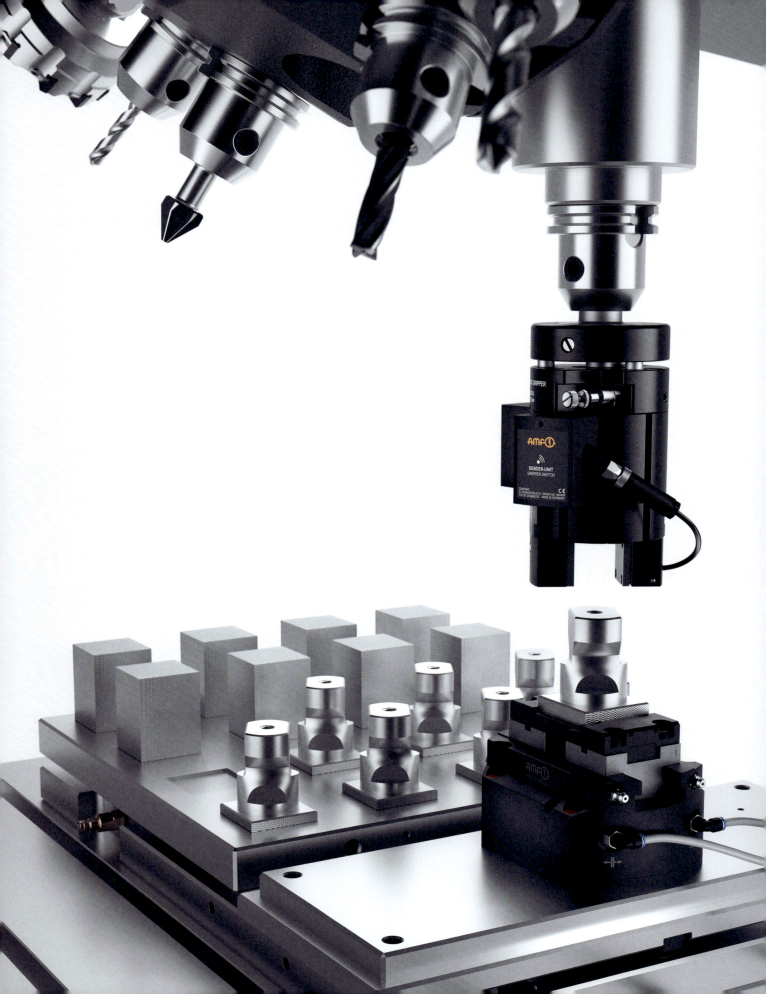

GOLD — 1650 — GREIFSYSTEM / GRIPPER SYSTEM

JURY STATEMENT

Der Greifer ist ein herausragendes Beispiel für ein B2B-Design, das rein funktionale Elemente verbessert. So präsentiert sich das multifunktionale System sehr sauber, klar gegliedert und kompakt. Dabei wird die Option, Sensoren individuell anzubauen, vorbildlich gelöst.

The gripper is an outstanding example of a B2B design that improves purely functional aspects. Accordingly, the multifunctional system makes a very neat, clearly structured and compact impression. The solution for the individual addition of optional sensors is exemplary.

HERSTELLER / MANUFACTURER
Andreas Maier GmbH & Co. KG
Fellbach

DESIGN
Inhouse

VERTRIEB / DISTRIBUTOR
Andreas Maier GmbH & Co. KG
Fellbach

Die Umstellung auf vollautomatische Bearbeitungsprozesse erfordert meist aufwendige Adaptionen der Maschinen oder gar deren Ersatz durch neue Anlagen. Das Greifsystem 1650 bietet dazu unter dem Stichwort Lean Automation eine kostengünstige Alternative. Modular aufgebaut, eignet sich das Greifsystem für die Nutzung in unterschiedlichsten Werkzeugmaschinen und wird wie ein konventionelles Werkzeug aus dem Magazin eingewechselt.

Konkret kann der Greifer mit seinen verschiedenen Einsätzen Werkstücke bis acht Kilogramm Gewicht umsetzen und zur Bearbeitung exakt positionieren.

Optional lässt sich das Greifsystem mit einer Funksensorik ausrüsten, die per Bluetooth Low-Energy-Daten über den aktuellen Status von Greifer und Werkstück in das Industrie 4.0-Netzwerk einspeist. Das Design des Greifers ermöglicht die einfache Addition dieser Sensoren und deren Justierung durch Fixierungsnuten entlang des Greifergehäuses.

Switching to fully automated machining processes usually calls for complex and costly adaptations to the machine tools or even their replacement with new equipment. The 1650 gripper system offers an inexpensive alternative under the heading of »lean automation«. The modularly designed gripper system is suitable for use in a wide range of machine tools and is unloaded from the magazine just like a conventional tool.

Specifically, the gripper and its various inserts can transport workpieces weighing up to 8 kilograms and position them exactly as required for machining.

The gripper system can also be equipped with an optional wireless sensing system that uses Bluetooth to enter low-energy data about the current status of the gripper and workpiece into the Industry 4.0 network. The gripper's design makes the addition of the sensors simple and allows them to be adjusted via slots in its housing.

DOMENICO FARINA DESIGNER,
ANDREAS MAIER GMBH & CO. KG

»Durch die Gestaltung bauen
wir Hemmschwellen ab.«

»Our goal is to overcome inhibitions
via the design.«

DOMENICO FARINA DESIGNER, ANDREAS MAIER GMBH & CO. KG

→ Auch wenn das Greifsystem automatisiert, also ohne menschlichen Kontakt arbeitet, zeigt es einen hohen ästhetischen Anspruch. Warum?
Bei der Produktgestaltung legen wir sowohl auf die Funktion als auch auf die Ästhetik Wert. Sehr viele AMF-Produkte haben im Einsatz kaum noch menschlichen Kontakt – nicht nur in der Automatisierung. Neben einer gesicherten Funktion beinhaltet ein gutes Design noch weitere Aspekte wie Formgestaltung und Bedienerfreundlichkeit. Diese Eigenschaften unterstützen den Anwender, zum Beispiel bei der Inbetriebnahme. Der Kunde kennt uns als verlässlichen Partner und Hersteller von Qualitätsprodukten. Das spiegelt sich auch in der Produktgestaltung wider und transportiert so unsere Markenwerte.

Welchen Spielraum konnten Sie beim Design dieses so technisch determinierten Produktes nutzen?
Automatisierung, Industrie 4.0 – das klingt für viele technisch sehr komplex. Durch die Gestaltung bauen wir Hemmschwellen ab. So sollte der Greifer ein schlichtes Erscheinungsbild erhalten, das sowohl technische Qualität ausstrahlt als auch ein einfaches Handling vermittelt. Technisch waren die Rahmenbedingungen durch den Systemgedanken, die engen Platzverhältnisse im Werkzeugmagazin, den effizienten Materialeinsatz und die optimierte Fertigung eng gesteckt. Ein eigenständiges, wiedererkennbares Design, das sich vom Wettbewerb absetzt und gut in das Erscheinungsbild von AMF passt, war dabei ebenso relevant.

Wann hat AMF das Design implementiert? Und wer entscheidet letztlich über das Design?
Das Design ist seit langer Zeit fester Bestandteil der Entwicklung bei AMF – seit einigen Jahren geht AMF den Weg mit einer Inhouse-Designabteilung. Durch diese engere Anbindung entsteht ein guter Austausch zwischen allen Beteiligten über den gesamten Entwicklungsprozess hinweg. Zudem habe ich als Inhouse-Designer einen Blick über das gesamte Produktsortiment der Firma. Entwurfsvarianten werden bei uns in bereichsübergreifenden Meetings präsentiert, diskutiert und entschieden.

Wie stärkt das Design die Position Ihres Unternehmens im Markt?
Gutes Design mit Wiedererkennungsmerkmalen ist für unsere Kunden ein wichtiges Zeichen für gleichbleibende Qualität – und gleichzeitig für AMF eine Stärkung der Marktposition. Zwar hat ein Techniker bei einem Investitionsgut in erster Linie nicht das Design im Blick, jedoch macht Design Funktion und Werte sichtbar. Gute technische Qualität, gepaart mit einem ansprechenden Design und wertvollen Produktdetails wird vom Kunden geschätzt und schafft Vertrauen.

Das 1890 als Andreas Maier Fellbach (AMF) gegründete Unternehmen ist heute ein Komplettanbieter in der Spanntechnik und gehört weltweit zu den Marktführern. AMF entwickelt Projektanfertigungen und Speziallösungen für Kund*innen sowie Standardlösungen, die sich am Markt durchsetzen. Mit mehr als 5.000 Produkten sowie zahlreichen Patenten gehören die Schwaben zu den Innovativsten ihrer Branche.

www.amf.de

→ Even though the gripper system automates processes, i.e. works without human contact, it nevertheless sets high aesthetic standards. Why?
When it comes to product design, we attach importance to both the function and the aesthetics. A great many AMF products hardly have any contact with humans at all when they're in use – and I don't just mean automation-related products. Besides ensuring the product functions reliably, a good design factors other aspects like the outer form and usability into the equation as well. Those are the features that provide support for the user, during setup for example. Our clients know us as a reliable partner and a manufacturer of quality products. Our product design reflects that, so it communicates our brand values as well.

How much freedom did you have when designing a product that's so heavily influenced by technical considerations?
Automation, Industry 4.0 – to a lot of people, that sounds like highly complex technology. Our goal is to overcome inhibitions like that via the design. That's why we wanted to give the gripper a simple appearance that not only visualises its technical quality but communicates that it's simple to use as well. As for the technical aspects, the system-based concept, the very limited amount of space available in the tool magazine, and objectives like the efficient use of materials and optimised production meant that we had to work within narrowly defined parameters. And last but not least, creating an independent, recognisable design that stands out from competitors and is a good fit with AMF's corporate design was just as relevant.

At what point did AMF bring design into the development process? And who has the final say about the design?
At AMF, design has been an integral part of development for a long time – and the company has been operating an in-house design department for several years now. That closer link gives rise to a good exchange of views and ideas between all those involved with the development process from beginning to end. Plus, as an in-house designer, I've got a good overview of the company's entire product range. Our approach is to present, discuss and decide on the different versions of the design at cross-departmental meetings.

How does design strengthen your company's market position?
For our clients, a good design with features that ensure brand recognition is an important sign of consistent quality – and strengthens AMF's market position at the same time. Although the design isn't top of a technician's mind when they're dealing with capital goods, it's the design that visualises the function and values. Good technical quality, paired with an appealing design and meaningful product details, are appreciated by the customer and inspire confidence.

Founded in 1890 under the name Andreas Maier Fellbach (AMF), today the company is a one-stop supplier for clamping technology and a global market leader in its field. AMF develops project-based and customised solutions, as well as standard products that enjoy widespread success on the market. With more than 5,000 products and numerous patents, the Baden-Württemberg company is one of the most innovative in its field.

www.amf.de

SILVER	STIFTSCHLÜSSEL	SET MIT HALTER
	→ SEITE / PAGE	SET WITH HOLDER
	30	

| SILVER | TAILORED BLANK LINE → SEITE / PAGE 31 | FERTIGUNGSLINIE PRODUCTION LINE |

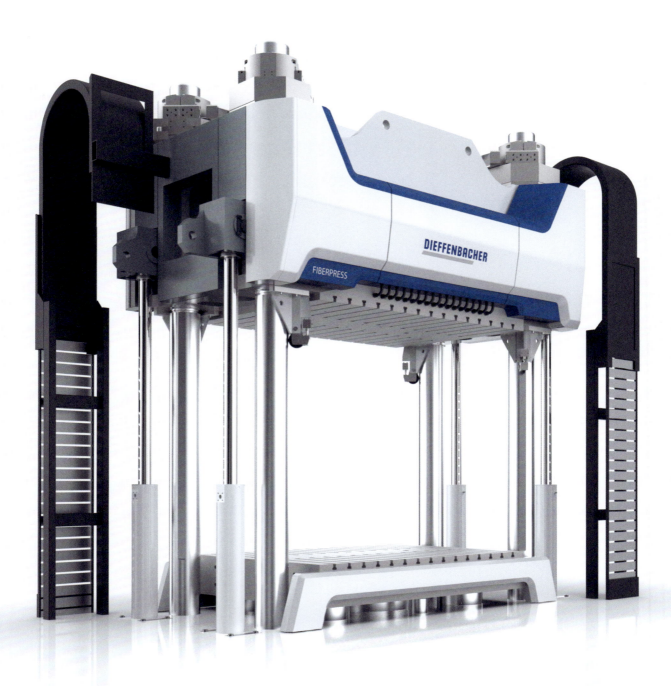

SILVER SMARTSOLUTIONS BEARBEITUNGSANLAGEN / MACHINING SYSTEMS
→ SEITE / PAGE 32

SILVER TUS / DN 100 ULTRASCHALL-GASMESSZÄHLER
ULTRASONIC GAS METER

→ SEITE / PAGE
33

SPECIAL MENTION — PROBOXX → SEITE / PAGE 34 — ISOLIERSTOFF-GEHÄUSE ENCLOSURE SERIES

SPECIAL MENTION

BIG INK XL

→ SEITE / PAGE 35

TIEFLOCHMARKER
DEEP HOLE MARKER

SILVER

STIFTSCHLÜSSEL — SET MIT HALTER / SET WITH HOLDER

JURY STATEMENT

Eigentlich sollte man meinen, an dem seit langem etablierten Sechskant-Stiftschlüssel ließe sich nichts mehr optimieren. Aber das Set beweist das Gegenteil: Es verbessert die Usability im täglichen Gebrauch wesentlich, die UV-Beschichtung reduziert den Schwund.

You could be forgiven for thinking that there's nothing left to optimise when it comes to such a well-established tool as the hexagonal L-key. This set proves the opposite: it improves everyday usability and minimises losses thanks to the UV-reactive coating.

HERSTELLER/MANUFACTURER
Wiha Werkzeuge GmbH
Schonach

DESIGN
Inhouse

VERTRIEB/DISTRIBUTOR
Wiha Werkzeuge GmbH
Schonach

Filigrane Sechskant-Stiftschlüssel werden gern vergessen, gehen verloren oder verschwinden im Dunkel hinter einer Maschine. Daher sind die Stifte dieses neunteiligen Sets in gut sichtbaren Signalfarben beschichtet, die zudem fluoreszieren, wenn sie mit einer UV-Lichtquelle beleuchtet werden. Auf einer Seite mit einer Kugelkopfform versehen, können die Schlüssel auch in Winkeln von bis zu 25 Grad angesetzt werden. Der Halter hält das Set kompakt beieinander, eine Klemmung verhindert das Herausfallen einzelner Schlüssel. Wird ein Schlüssel gedreht, so fächert sich das ganze Set im Halter für besseren Zugriff auf.

It's not unusual for slender hex keys to be left behind, get lost or disappear in the darkness behind a machine. That's why the keys in this nine-piece set are painted in bright, easily identifiable colours that fluoresce when illuminated with a UV light source. Equipped with a ball end on one side, the keys can be positioned at an angle of up to 25 degrees. The holder keeps the set together in compact form and is equipped with a clamping mechanism to prevent individual keys from falling out. If one key is twisted, the entire set fans out in the holder for better access.

SILVER — TAILORED BLANK LINE / FERTIGUNGSLINIE PRODUCTION LINE

JURY STATEMENT

Es ist nicht einfach, konstruktiv so unterschiedlichen Maschinen ein gemeinsames Erscheinungsbild zu verleihen. Hier ist es aber gut gelungen. Jede Maschine zeigt ihre besondere Funktion, verbindet sich aber dennoch optisch mit ihren Nachbarn.

It isn't easy to create an overarching look for machines that are constructed so differently. In this case, however, the endeavour has been successful. Each machine indicates its specific function while nevertheless sharing visual features with its neighbours.

HERSTELLER/MANUFACTURER
Dieffenbacher GmbH
Eppingen

DESIGN
Defortec GmbH
Dettenhausen

VERTRIEB/DISTRIBUTOR
Dieffenbacher GmbH
Eppingen

Die Fertigungslinie mit ihren drei Maschinen bildet den automatisierten Produktionsprozess von Bauteilen aus thermoplastischen Fasermaterialien komplett ab. Für das Legen der Tapes ist die Fiberforge zuständig, Fibercon homogenisiert das Gelege thermisch und die Fiberpress übernimmt schließlich die dreidimensionale, werkzeugbasierte Verformung. Das Design zielte darauf ab, diese drei völlig unterschiedlich aufgebauten Anlagen formal zusammenzufassen. Neben dem durchgehenden Thema der Fase spielt hier die Farbigkeit eine große Rolle: Die CI-Farben Weiß und Blau stehen im Vordergrund, während sekundäre Bereiche durchgängig in Hell- oder Dunkelgrau gefasst sind.

With its three machines, the production line maps the entire automated production process for components made of thermoplastic fibre materials. The Fiberforge lays the tape, the Fibercon machine homogenises the lay-ups thermally and the Fiberpress forms the three-dimensional, die-based part. The design aimed to find a shared language of form for the three machines, which are totally different in structure. Besides the common theme of chamfered edges, colour plays a major role as well: the focus is on the CI colours white and blue, with light or dark grey for secondary areas.

SILVER   **SMARTSOLUTIONS**   **BEARBEITUNGSANLAGEN / MACHINING SYSTEMS**

> **JURY STATEMENT**
>
> So könnte Industrie 4.0 gelingen. Dank des visuell und intuitiv erfassbaren Interfaces können auch ungeschulte Mitarbeiter*innen die Einrichtung der Prozesse übernehmen. Das ist ein Paradebeispiel für hohe Nutzerfreundlichkeit im B2B-Bereich.
>
> This is the kind of design that could make Industry 4.0 succeed. Thanks to the visually and intuitively accessible interface, even untrained employees can set up the processes. This is a prime example of excellent usability in the B2B sector.

HERSTELLER / MANUFACTURER
Hahn Automation GmbH
Rheinböllen

DESIGN
Dreikant
Weimar

VERTRIEB / DISTRIBUTOR
Hahn Automation GmbH
Rheinböllen

Die Produktfamilie besteht aus drei Maschinen mit identischem Volumen und Design, aber unterschiedlichen Funktionen. Gedacht für die Kleinserienfertigung oder den Einsatz im Labor können so Sprühdosierung, Einpressen und Verschrauben in automatisierten, modularen Prozessen abgebildet werden. Die Konfiguration erfolgt am Tablet mit einer eigens entwickelten, intuitiv nutzbaren Software, die keine Programmierkenntnisse verlangt, sondern auf Grafiken und Symbolen basiert. Über die intelligente Menüführung werden Nutzer*innen Schritt für Schritt durch den Einrichtungsprozess geleitet. Die Benutzeroberfläche erinnert dabei an das gewohnte Bild eines Smartphones.

The product family consists of three machines with an identical volume and design but different functions. Intended for small-scale production or laboratory use, they map spray dispensing, pressing and screwing in automated, modular processes. The system is configured via a tablet with specially developed, intuitive software based on graphics and symbols – no programming knowledge is required. The intelligent menu navigation guides users through the setup process step by step. The user interface resembles the familiar appearance of a smartphone.

SILVER TUS / DN 100 ULTRASCHALL-GASMESSZÄHLER
ULTRASONIC GAS METER

JURY STATEMENT

Mit seinem filigranen Design und der weißen Farbgebung ragt der Gaszähler maximal aus der eher von massiven Leitungen geprägten Umgebung heraus – und präsentiert selbstbewusst den technologischen Anspruch des Herstellers. Herausfordernd für das Designkonzept dürfte gewesen sein, dass es für unterschiedliche Rohrdurchmesser skalierbar sein muss.

With its subtle design and white colouring, the gas flow meter stands out prominently from its surroundings, which tend to be dominated by massive pipelines – thereby self-confidently presenting the manufacturer's technological expertise. The fact that the meter has to be scalable in order to accommodate different pipe diameters must have been a particularly challenging objective for the design concept.

Statt eines mechanisch arbeitenden Durchflusszählers misst dieses Gerät das durchströmende Gas mittels eines Ultraschallsensors – ein für diesen Produktbereich neues Verfahren mit minimalen Wartungsanforderungen. Der Zähler vermittelt diese Neuerung durch die spannende Kombination aus Taillierungen, überspannten Flächen, präzisen Kanten und weichen Flächenübergängen. Zudem zielt das global gedachte Design auf eine hohe Wiedererkennung ab, um den Zähler samt seinem Hersteller im Kontext der harten On- und Offshore-Anwendungen klar erkennbar zu machen. Das sparsame Display unterstützt lediglich Wartungsarbeiten vor Ort, die eigentliche Steuerung, Überwachung und Messwertübermittlung erfolgt per Anbindung an das Internet.

Instead of a mechanical meter, this device uses an ultrasonic sensor to measure the gas flow – a new method for this product category with minimal maintenance requirements. The meter visualises this technical innovation with an intriguing combination of waisted forms, domed surfaces, precise edges and soft transitions. In addition, the design – which is intended for a global clientele – aims to ensure high recognition so as to create a strong visual identity for both the meter and its manufacturer in the context of tough on- and offshore applications. The economical display only supports on-site maintenance; regulation, monitoring and data transmission functions are enabled via the internet.

HERSTELLER / MANUFACTURER
Goldcard Smart Group Co. Ltd.
Hangzhou
China

DESIGN
Code2Design
Ostfildern

VERTRIEB / DISTRIBUTOR
Metreg Technologies GmbH
Fürstenwalde

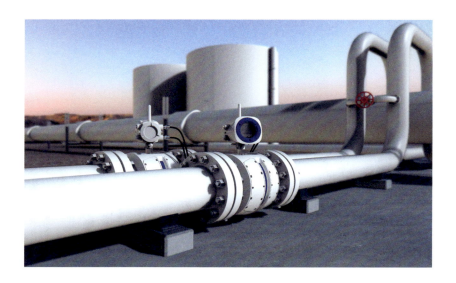

SPECIAL MENTION   PROBOXX   ISOLIERSTOFF-GEHÄUSE
ENCLOSURE SERIES

JURY STATEMENT

Klar und aufgeräumt gestaltet, nimmt sich das Gehäuse gegenüber den implantierbaren Schaltern zurück und betont diese. Das ist klassisches Industriedesign wie aus dem Lehrbuch. Auch, weil zugleich Betriebssicherheit und Montage verbessert wurden.

With its clear and uncluttered design, the enclosure accentuates the implantable switches rather than competing with them. A textbook example of classic industrial design – partly also because it improves safety and mounting at the same time.

HERSTELLER/MANUFACTURER
Georg Schlegel GmbH & Co. KG
Dürmentingen

DESIGN
Ottenwälder und Ottenwälder
Schwäbisch Gmünd

VERTRIEB/DISTRIBUTOR
Georg Schlegel GmbH & Co. KG
Dürmentingen

Ein bis vier Taster, Schalter oder Not-Halte lassen sich in dieses robuste Kunststoffgehäuse einsetzen, das universell nutzbar für Steuerungen von Maschinen- oder Industrieanlagen ist. Der Betrieb ist sowohl mit konventioneller Verkabelung als auch mit Feldbus- oder Funksystemen möglich. Dank des neuen Befestigungsprinzips kann das Gehäuse auch auf Standard-Profilschienen montiert werden, ohne dass es geöffnet werden muss. Die eigentliche Verschraubung des Gehäuses befindet sich an seiner Unterseite, somit lässt es sich nur nach Demontage öffnen – die Sichtseite bleibt derweil optisch aufgeräumt, nichts lenkt von den Bedienelementen ab.

The robust plastic enclosure can be equipped with one to four pushbuttons, switches or emergency stops and is universally suitable for use with the controls of industrial plant or machinery. It can be used both with conventional wiring and with fieldbus or radio systems. Thanks to the new fixing principle, the enclosure can even be mounted on standard rails without having to be opened. The actual screw connection is at the bottom of the enclosure so that it can only be opened when dismounted – leaving the visible side neat and tidy with nothing to distract from the control elements.

SPECIAL MENTION — BIG INK XL — TIEFLOCHMARKER / DEEP HOLE MARKER

JURY STATEMENT

Der Marker löst ein praktisches und alltägliches Montageproblem auf höchst professionelle Art. Mit seiner langen Spitze lassen sich exakte Markierungen in der Tiefe eines Bauteils setzen, zugleich ist er universell für viele andere Kennzeichnungen nutzbar.

The marker provides a highly professional solution to a practical problem that fitters encounter on a daily basis. Thanks to its long tip, it can be used to make precise markings through deep holes, but is also universally suitable for many other types of markings.

HERSTELLER / MANUFACTURER
Pica-Marker GmbH
Kirchehrenbach

DESIGN
Winkelbauer-Design
Ludwigsburg
und / and
Inhouse
Stephan Möck

VERTRIEB / DISTRIBUTOR
Pica-Marker GmbH
Kirchehrenbach

Wer montiert, muss markieren. Zum Beispiel eine Bohrung, eine Schnittkante, ein Zeichen zum Ablängen. Eine einfache Übung, eigentlich. Doch wenn es darum geht, durch ein zu montierendes, dickes Bauteil hindurch eine Bohrung anzuzeichnen, wird es mitunter schwierig. Abhilfe schafft der Tieflochmarker mit seiner langen Spitze. Gedacht für den professionellen Einsatz, ist dieses hilfreiche Werkzeug auf Langlebigkeit und schnelles Handling hin optimiert. Es ruht in einem in der Hosentasche sicher fixierten Köcher, lässt sich einhändig entnehmen und setzt eine exakte Markierung mit sofort wasser- und wischfester Tinte. Die Spitze lässt sich wenden, die Tinte nachfüllen.

If you're fitting something, you have to mark things. A drill hole, for instance, a cutting line, or to indicate where something has to trimmed. Essentially, a simple exercise. But sometimes, when you have to mark a drill hole through a thick part that you want to attach, it can be more difficult. Thanks to its long tip, this deep hole marker provides a solution. Intended for professional use, the helpful tool has been optimised for a long life and quick handling. It rests in a quiver that's securely attached to a trouser pocket, can be removed with one hand and makes a precise marking with ink that is instantly waterproof and smudgeproof. The nib can be turned around and the marker is refillable.

META
TECHNOLOGIE-
UMSETZUNG

FELDSCHWARM
FSE II

AUTONOME AGRARMASCHINE
AUTONOMOUS AGRICULTURAL MACHINERY

FELDSCHWARM
FSE II

AUTONOME
AGRARMASCH

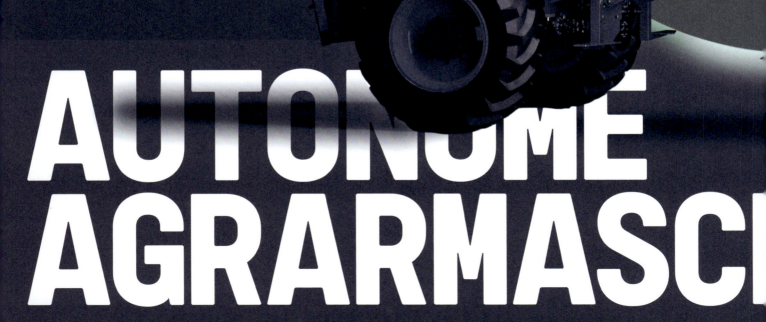

INVESTITIONSGÜTER, WERKZEUGE
CAPITAL GOODS, TOOLS

META
CHNOLOGIE—
UMSETZUNG

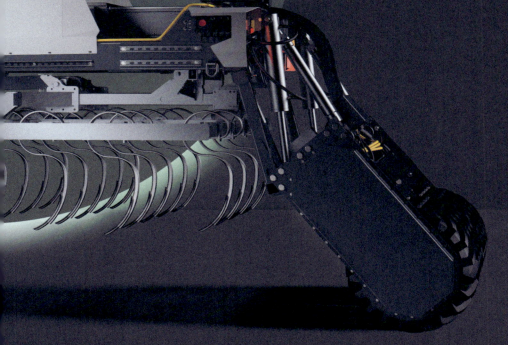

INE

META TECHNOLOGIE-UMSETZUNG

FELDSCHWARM FSE II
AUTONOME AGRARMASCHINE / AUTONOMOUS AGRICULTURAL MACHINERY

JURY STATEMENT

Noch befinden sich Agrar-Roboter im Versuchsstadium, aber in wenigen Jahren werden sie wohl Alltag sein. Feldschwarm ist ein extrem technologiegetriebenes Verbundprojekt, bei dem das Design von Beginn an einbezogen war. Der Gestaltungsanspruch ist ausgesprochen hoch, schließt alle Details der Maschine sowie die Nutzer*innen ein und verleiht dem Ganzen einen klaren, visionären Charakter. Das Design visualisiert die enorme Wurfweite dieses Projekts.

Agricultural robots are still in the experimental stage for the time being but will probably be part of everyday life in just a few years from now. Feldschwarm is an extremely technology-driven joint project that factored in the design right from the start. The design is of exceptionally high quality; it encompasses every detail of the machine as well as its users and gives the entire concept a clear, visionary overall character that visualises the enormous scope of the project's potential.

HERSTELLER/MANUFACTURER
Feldschwarm Konsortium
Dresden

DESIGN
Technisches Design TU Dresden
Dresden

Steigende Nachfrage, schrumpfende Anbauflächen, Personalmangel und klimatische Veränderungen setzen die globale Landwirtschaft unter starken Innovationsdruck. Autonom in Schwärmen agierende Maschinen könnten schon bald das Bild auf den Feldern bestimmen. Wie, das zeigt das interdisziplinäre Forschungsprojekt Feldschwarm, an dem elf Partner aus Industrie und Forschung beteiligt sind.

Als konkretes Ergebnis entstand dabei FSE II, eine autonome Bearbeitungsmaschine, deren Werkzeuge nicht mehr angehängt werden, sondern sich zwischen den Achsen befinden. Damit wird die Maschine schmaler, leichter und modularer. Das Design konzentriert sich auf den Maschinenkopf mit der Antriebseinheit und integriert die Sensorik sowie Lichtelemente, mit denen die Maschine kommuniziert. Die Landwirtin oder der Landwirt steuert den Schwarm über ein Tablet und ein grafisches User-Interface.

Growing demand, shrinking cropland, labour shortages and climate change are putting global agriculture under immense pressure to innovate. Before long, swarms of autonomous machines could well be shaping the face of arable land. Feldschwarm (Field Swarm), an interdisciplinary project involving 11 partners from industry and research, shows how.

FSE II is a concrete outcome of the project – an autonomous machine with tools that are incorporated between its axles rather than being attached to the back of the vehicle. That makes the machine narrower, lighter and more modular. The design focuses on the machine head with drive unit and integrates both the sensor technology and illuminated elements that the machine uses to communicate. The farmer controls the swarm via a tablet and graphical user interface.

FOCUS OPEN META
Der Focus Meta zeichnet Produkte aus, die beispielhafte Lösungsansätze für ein übergeordnetes und aktuelles gestalterisches, technisches oder gesellschaftliches Thema aufzeigen. Die Jury verleiht diese Auszeichnung unabhängig von den Produktkategorien – und sie wählt auch das konkrete Thema des Focus Open Meta.

FOCUS OPEN META
The Focus Meta award honours products that feature exemplary solution strategies for addressing the design-related, technical or societal challenges relating to a current and overarching issue. The jury presents this award independently of the product categories. It also selects the specific topic of the Focus Open Meta.

JENS KRZYWINSKI — PROFESSOR TECHNISCHES DESIGN, TU DRESDEN

»Bei interdisziplinären Fragestellungen sind wir Designer dank unseren großen Schnittstellen-Kompetenzen ideale Innovationspartner.«

»When it comes to interdisciplinary questions, we designers make ideal innovation partners thanks to our considerable interfacing skills.«

JENS KRZYWINSKI — PROFESSOR OF TECHNICAL DESIGN, TU DRESDEN

→ **As a designer, what position and how much weight did you have within the development team?**

We were on board all the way from the initial sketch to the test in the field and were involved with building up the development team as time went on. Because the project was completely new and therefore not that easy to understand, our visualisations and demonstrations were hugely important for creating a basis for internal communication with the participating SMEs from the region. When it comes to interdisciplinary questions, our considerable interfacing skills mean that we designers make ideal innovation partners for initiating and pushing ahead with new approaches.

How much can or should the form of an autonomous agricultural robot distance itself from that of the traditional tractor?

The vehicle concept enables us to arrange the components in a new way, which obviously influences the design language just as much as the modular principle does. On the other hand, its performance and traction are definitely comparable with a tractor, which results in a similar size. What's more, in order for it to gain acceptance within the agricultural sector, it's important for the vehicle to look very robust and show that it can cope with the tough everyday conditions on a farm. On the other hand, it shouldn't hide its hi-tech credentials. And thirdly, we need to think about the people who drive to the countryside and encounter an unmanned robot: the design needs to win their trust and communicate visually via light signals.

And when can we expect to see the first vehicles in the fields?

The prototype is ready to go in terms of driving capability, however the AI and complex navigation still need further development. Up until now we've invested a great deal of energy in the technological concept, next it will be a case of verifying it in agricultural practice. Besides acceptance, that also involves such simple-sounding aspects as cleaning the machines. We're in the process of raising funds for this phase of the project.

What will the farmer do without his tractor?

He can keep his favourite tractor, of course, but he'll use it differently. Rather than just pulling machinery, it could serve as the control centre for his fleet of robots and a mobile office, for instance.

The chair of technical design at TU Dresden has been working on the Feldschwarm (Field Swarm) project for more than four years. A total of seven companies and four research institutes are involved with the basic development of autonomous and swarm-based field robots. The project is sponsored by Germany's Federal Ministry of Education and Research.

www.feldschwarm.de
https://tu-dresden.de/ing/maschinenwesen/imm/td

GERRIT TERSTIEGE — DESIGNJOURNALIST UND TEXTER, FREIBURG / DESIGN JOURNALIST AND AUTHOR, FREIBURG

»Im Design geht es um Details, die man am realen Objekt am besten beurteilen kann. Beim Focus Open kann man all dies in Ruhe prüfen und miteinander diskutieren. Das macht die Jurierung so besonders.«

»Design is about details, and the best way to judge them is to experience the real, physical object. With Focus Open, there's plenty of time to inspect and discuss everything. That's what makes the judging so special.«

Gerrit Terstiege, lange Jahre Chefredakteur der Designzeitschrift form, schreibt heute über Kunst, Design, Literatur und Musik in Art, Galore, Mint, Rolling Stone und Monopol sowie für Design-Unternehmen und -Hochschulen. Er war Gastprofessor an der FH Mainz und der HfG Karlsruhe. Im Birkhäuser Verlag sind drei von Terstiege herausgegebene Bücher zur Design-Theorie- und Praxis erschienen. Er führte zahlreiche Interviews mit namhaften Designerinnen und Designern, darunter Konstantin Grcic, Alessandro Mendini, Alexander Neumeister und Ettore Sottsass.

After many years as editor-in-chief of design magazine »form«, Gerrit Terstiege currently writes about art, design, literature and music in publications such as Art, Galore, Mint, Rolling Stone and Monopol, as well as for design companies, colleges and universities. He has been a visiting professor at Mainz University of Applied Sciences and Karlsruhe University of Arts and Design. Terstiege has edited three books on design theory and practice published by Birkhäuser Verlag. He has conducted numerous interviews with renowned designers, including Konstantin Grcic, Alessandro Mendini, Alexander Neumeister and Ettore Sottsass.

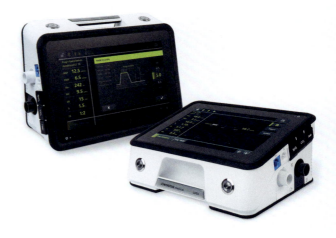

1 → SEITE / PAGE
48–53

2 → SEITE / PAGE
54–59

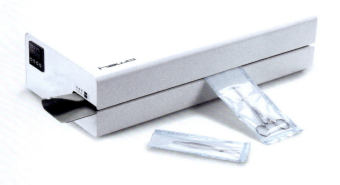

3 → SEITE / PAGE
60

HEALTHCARE
HEALTHCARE

GOLD:
1 **LYTE**
Invacare International GmbH
Witterswil
Schweiz/Switzerland

2 **LUISA**
Löwenstein Medical Technology
GmbH & Co. KG
Hamburg

SILVER:
3 **HD 650 ECOPAK**
Hawo GmbH
Obrigheim

Wer medizinische Geräte gestaltet, bewegt sich in einem besonders sensiblen Bereich und übernimmt große soziale Verantwortung für Patient*innen wie auch für das medizinische Personal. Neben Produkten für die klinische Akutversorgung verlangen auch barriereabbauende Geräte und Hilfsmittel für Personen mit eingeschränkten Möglichkeiten oder chronischen Problemen ausgefeilte Gestaltungskonzepte.

Designers of medical equipment operate in a particularly sensitive area and have a high level of social responsibility towards patients and medical staff alike. That calls for sophisticated design concepts – not just for products for acute clinical care, but for devices, aids and appliances that tackle the barriers faced by people with certain impairments or chronic problems too.

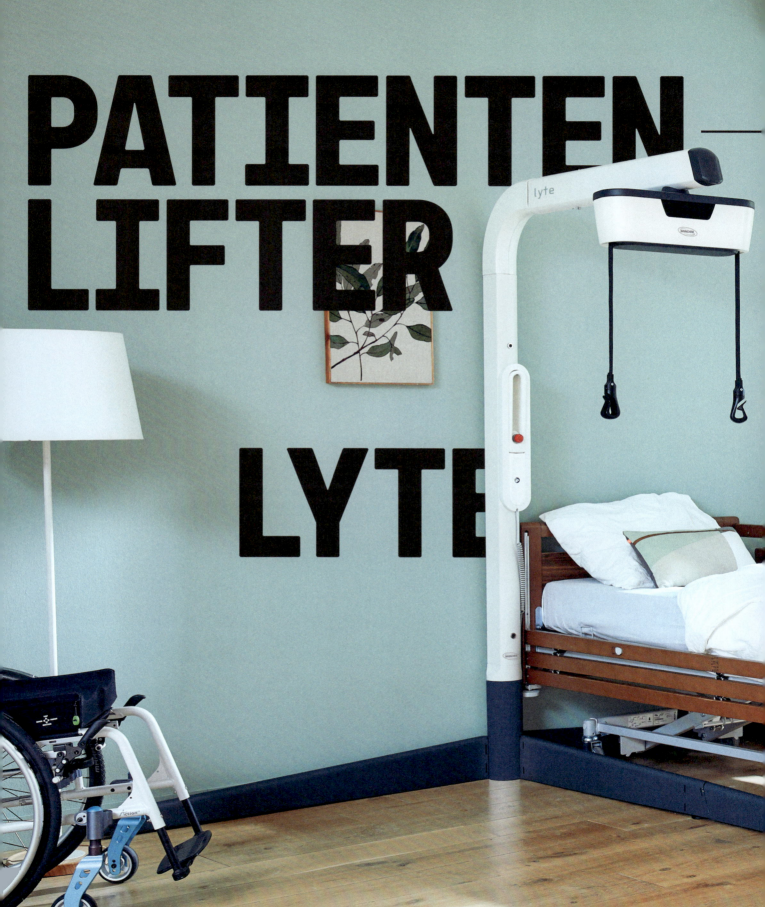

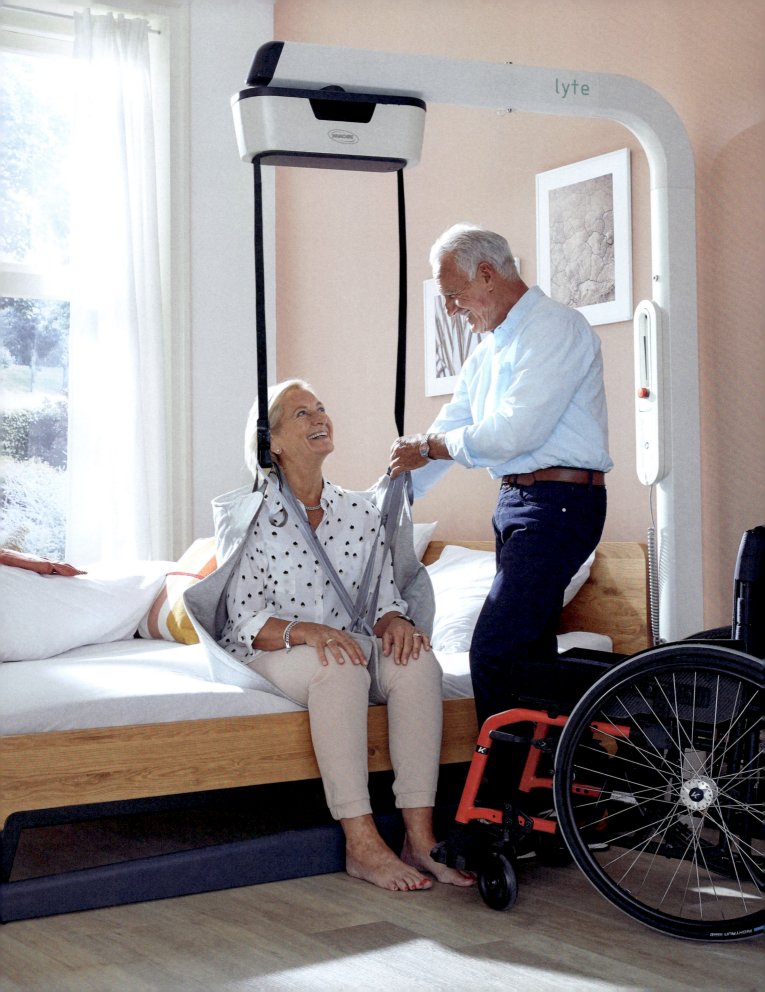

GOLD — LYTE — PATIENTENLIFTER / PATIENT LIFTER

JURY STATEMENT

Ein sehr wichtiges Produkt, das wertvolle Impulse für die heimische Pflege bringt. Das neue, ästhetisch motivierte Konzept wirkt nicht stigmatisierend und löst mit seiner freien Platzierbarkeit viele Probleme herkömmlicher Patientenlifter. Eine saubere Gestaltung für ein schwieriges Marktsegment.

A very important product that provides valuable impetus for at-home care. The new, aesthetically motivated concept is not stigmatising and, because it can be positioned anywhere, solves many of the problems associated with conventional patient lifters. An immaculate design for a difficult segment of the market.

HERSTELLER/MANUFACTURER
Invacare International GmbH
Witterswil
Schweiz/Switzerland

DESIGN
UP Designstudio GmbH & Co. KG
Stuttgart

VERTRIEB/DISTRIBUTOR
Invacare International GmbH
Witterswil
Schweiz/Switzerland

Die Pflege von Menschen in ihrem normalen Umfeld ist eine Herausforderung, die entsprechender Hilfsmittel bedarf. Dazu gehören Patientenlifter für das Umsetzen von mobilitätseingeschränkten Menschen, meist vom Bett in den Rollstuhl und umgekehrt. Ihre rein technische Anmutung lassen verfügbare Lifter allerdings wie Fremdkörper in der Wohnumgebung wirken. Lyte präsentiert sich hingegen mit einer Formgebung und einer Materialität, die dem Gerät einen Möbelcharakter verleiht. Drei schlanke Streben stützen den Lifter am Boden ab. Die Hebearbeit übernimmt eine elektrische, mit integrierter Waage ausgestattete Winde. Sie ist verdrehbar am filigranen Ausleger montiert und lässt sich via Kabel-Fernbedienung aktivieren. Das Bedienkonzept ist bewusst einfach gehalten, so wird der Ausleger über einen großen Griff manuell gedreht. Lyte erfordert kein Spezialbett, er ist direkt daneben und ohne zusätzliche Fixierungen nutzbar.

Caring for people in their normal environment is a challenge that calls for appropriate aids, such as patient lifters for transferring people with limited mobility, usually from bed to a wheelchair and back again. However, the lifters available have a purely technical appearance that makes them look totally out of place in a home setting. Lyte is different – thanks to a design and materials that give the equipment a furniture-like character. The lifter is supported by three slim struts that rest on the floor. The actual lifting is done by an electric hoist equipped with an integrated scale. It is swivel-mounted on the slender boom and activated via wired remote control. The controls have been kept deliberately simple: the boom, for instance, is turned manually using a large handle. Rather than being used in combination with a special bed, Lyte can be positioned right next to an ordinary bed without any additional fixings.

STEFAN LIPPERT   GESCHÄFTSFÜHRER,
UP DESIGNSTUDIO GMBH & CO. KG

»Lyte ist für ein alleine und weitgehend selbstständig lebendes, älteres Paar gedacht.«

»Lyte is intended for an elderly couple that lives alone and is largely independent.«

STEFAN LIPPERT — **MANAGING DIRECTOR, UP DESIGNSTUDIO GMBH & CO. KG**

→ **Normalerweise erinnern Patientenlifter eher an Hebegeräte in Werkstätten. Nicht so der Lyte – warum?**
Wir sollten ein klassisches Reha-Produkt ganz neu definieren und haben uns angesehen, was der Markt bisher so bietet. Das war sehr ernüchternd, die Patientenlifter sehen in der Regel aus wie Hebegeräte für den Motorwechsel. Will man damit eine Person aus dem Bett in den Rollstuhl umsetzen – das ist das Standardszenario – ist es nötig, das Hebegerät zu rangieren. Das scheitert meist an Schwellen, Teppichen oder an der fehlenden Kraft der bedienenden Person. Also haben wir einen einfachen, ortsfesten Lifter konzipiert.

Welchen Use Case hatten Sie bei der Entwicklung vor Augen?
Lyte ist für ein alleine und weitgehend selbstständig lebendes, älteres Paar gedacht. Allerdings ist ein Partner pflegebedürftig und auf die Hilfe des anderen angewiesen. Und diese pflegende Person wiederum benötigt ihrerseits Unterstützung im Alltag. Zum Beispiel beim täglichen Heraushebern aus dem Bett, das so kraftschonend, einfach und so platzsparend wie möglich sein soll. Und das, ohne aufwendige Umbauten am Bett oder im Raum vornehmen zu müssen.

Das Grundprinzip des Lyte ist bewusst einfach gehalten – warum?
Das hat gleich mehrere Gründe. Zunächst sollte das Gerät ganz einfach zu bedienen sein, also wirklich intuitiv. Daher gibt es nur eine Taste, die den Motor für das Heben und Senken aktiviert. Das Drehen des Auslegers erfolgt per Hand, mittels eines großen Griffs, der als unterstützender Hebel wirkt. Alles ist nachvollziehbar.

Auf der anderen Seite sieht das Lyte-Geschäftsmodell vor, dass der Lifter von der Kundschaft direkt am späteren Einsatzort getestet werden kann. Dazu muss das Gerät zerlegt von einer Person transportierbar und in maximal einer Stunde aufgebaut sein. All das haben wir während der Entwicklung sowohl mit Nutzer*innen, Pflegepersonal als auch den Vertriebs-Mitarbeiter*innen ausgetestet.

Was war die größte Herausforderung der Entwicklung?
Das Projekt in seiner Summe. Denn es ging ja darum, sowohl einen wachsenden Markt mit einem neuartigen, niedrigschwelligen Produkt zu erschließen als auch ein neues Geschäftsmodell auf die Schiene zu bringen und das alles konsequent zusammenzuführen. Am Ende sollte ein wirklich neues, schlankes Ergebnis stehen. Daher haben wir die geltenden Erstattungsrichtlinien zunächst bewusst nicht beachtet.

Das UP Designstudio mit Sitz in Stuttgart wurde in der Vergangenheit bereits mehrfach mit dem Focus Open ausgezeichnet – für Consumer-Produkte ebenso wie für Investitionsgüter. 1994 gegründet, firmierte das Büro lange Jahre als ipdd, seit 2017 ist es als UP Designstudio präsent. Geleitet wird das Studio von Stefan Lippert und Wolf Leonhardt.

www.updesignstudio.de

→ **Patient lifters are normally more like the kind of lifting device you'd expect to see at a car repair shop. The Lyte is different – why?**
We were asked to totally redefine a classic rehab product and took a look at what the market has to offer. It was very sobering: as a rule, the patient lifters look like the kind of thing you'd use to heave the engine out of a car. If you want to transfer somebody from their bed to a wheelchair – that's the standard scenario – you have to manoeuvre the lifter. That normally doesn't work too well due to thresholds or carpets or because the person using it lacks the strength. So we came up with a concept for a simple, stationary lift instead.

What use case did you have in mind during the development phase?
Lyte is intended for an elderly couple that lives alone and is largely independent. However, one of the partners needs care and depends on the help of the other. And the person doing the caring needs everyday support too. With getting their spouse out of bed every day, for instance – the whole procedure should be as effortless, simple and space-saving as possible. And it shouldn't require any complicated alterations to the bed or room either.

The basic principle behind the Lyte is deliberately simple – why?
There are several reasons for that. First, the device was to be very simple to use – really intuitive. That's why there's only one button, which activates the motor for raising and lowering the person being transferred. The boom is turned manually using a large handle that doubles as an auxiliary lever. Everything is easy to understand.

On the other hand, the Lyte business model is designed to let customers test the lift in the exact setting where it will eventually be used. That means it has to be possible for one person to transport it when it's disassembled and set it up again – within an hour at the very most. We tried all that out during the development stage – with the help of users, professional carers and the sales team.

What was the greatest challenge the development confronted you with?
The project as a whole: it wasn't just about tapping into a growing market with an innovative, low-threshold product; it was also a case of getting a new business model off the ground and bringing the whole thing together in a logical, consistent way. The ultimate goal was to end up with a genuinely new, lean result. That's why, to begin with, we made a conscious decision not to take the reimbursement guidelines into consideration.

UP Designstudio is based in Stuttgart and has won several Focus Open awards in the past – for both consumer products and capital goods. Founded in 1994, the firm operated as ipdd for many years before changing its name to UP Designstudio in 2017. The studio is headed by Stefan Lippert and Wolf Leonhardt.

www.updesignstudio.de

GOLD | LUISA | MOBILES BEATMUNGSGERÄT
MOBILE VENTILATOR

MOBILES BEATMUNGSGERÄT

HEALTHCARE
HEALTHCARE

LUISA

FOCUS GOLD

JURY STATEMENT

Das ist Medical Design par excellence, weil das Gerät die Lebensqualität vieler Menschen verbessert. Trotz des hohen technischen Komplexitätsgrades lässt es sich durch die Nutzer*innen einfach handhaben – dazu trägt das große, durch eine umlaufende Gummierung geschützte Display erheblich bei.

This is medical design par excellence because the device improves a great many people's quality of life. Despite the high degree of technical complexity, it is nevertheless simple to use – due in no small part to the large display, the edges of which are protected by a rubber trim.

HERSTELLER/MANUFACTURER
Löwenstein Medical Technology
GmbH & Co. KG
Hamburg

DESIGN
Inhouse
Anne Wonsyld
und/and
Stephan Kommunikationsdesign
Karlsruhe

VERTRIEB/DISTRIBUTOR
Löwenstein Medical Technology
GmbH & Co. KG
Hamburg

Menschen, die auf externe Beatmungshilfen angewiesen sind, haben dadurch oft Probleme, am normalen Leben teilzuhaben. Es sei denn, ein netzunabhängiges Beatmungsgerät steht zur Verfügung, das kompakt und damit alltagstauglich ist. Luisa schließt diese bisherige Lücke. Die mobile Beatmungshilfe lässt sich platzoptimiert stehend wie auch liegend nutzen, wird 18 Stunden lang von Batterien versorgt und ist auch für Outdoor-Aktivitäten geeignet. Das 3,8 Kilogramm schwere Gerät wird über einen farbigen 10-Zoll-Touchscreen bedient. Die Menüführung über das Display führt die Nutzer*innen intuitiv durch die Einstellungen und präsentiert schnell den aktuellen Status. Fehlfunktionen oder Probleme aktivieren einen Alarm, der wahlweise auch in einer zweiten Sprache ausgegeben werden kann. Luisa eignet sich für Erwachsene ebenso wie für Kinder und kann – als einziges Gerät seiner Art – adapterlos mit den drei international etablierten Schlauchsystemen verbunden werden.

People who depend on external breathing aids often find it difficult to participate in daily life. Unless, that is, they have a ventilator that doesn't have to be plugged in and is compact enough to be compatible with everyday activities – a gap that Luisa now fills. The mobile ventilator can be used in a space-saving upright position or horizontally, is powered by batteries for up to 18 hours and is also suitable for outdoor activities. The device weighs 3.8 kilograms and is operated via a 10-inch colour touchscreen with an intuitive interface that guides the user through the settings and quickly displays the current status. Malfunctions or problems activate an alarm that can be displayed in a second language if required. Luisa is suitable for both adults and children and is the only device of its kind that can be used with the three internationally established tube systems without the need for an adapter.

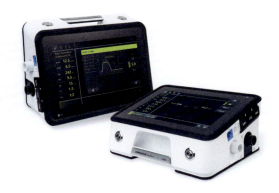

ANNE WONSYLD DESIGNERIN, LÖWENSTEIN MEDICAL TECHNOLOGY GMBH & CO. KG

»Insgesamt ging es uns darum, dem Thema Beatmung durch klares reduziertes Design die Komplexität und den Anwendern die Berührungsängste zu nehmen.«

»Our overall goal was to create a clear, minimalist design that takes the complexity out of ventilation and overcomes users' reservations.«

ANNE WONSYLD — DESIGNER, LÖWENSTEIN MEDICAL TECHNOLOGY GMBH + CO. KG

→ Covid-19 hat uns allen vor Augen geführt, wie wichtig Beatmungsgeräte sind. Wobei Luisa ja für andere Anwendungsszenarien entwickelt wurde.

Luisa ist ein lebenserhaltendes Beatmungsgerät sowohl für beatmungspflichtige Erwachsene als auch Kinder mit unterschiedlichsten Krankheitsbildern, hauptsächlich geht es dabei um neuromuskuläre Erkrankungen. Luisa kommt sowohl im häuslichen als auch im klinischen Bereich zum Einsatz.

Medizingeräte sind Langfrist-Projekte. Wann begann die Entwicklung von Luisa – und welche Prämissen standen dabei im Vordergrund?

Im ersten Schritt haben wir uns klar gemacht, welche Erwartungen Patienten, Ärzte, Pflegekräfte sowie Angehörige überhaupt an ein neues Beatmungsgerät in dieser Klasse stellen und wie die Nutzungsszenarien aussehen. Das war 2017. Unser Ansatz war, Luisa möglichst mobil, kompakt und einfach nutzbar zu machen. Der letzte Aspekt ist aus Sicherheitsgründen wichtig: Lässt sich ein Beatmungsgerät intuitiv und unkompliziert bedienen, sind viele potenzielle Fehlerquellen eliminiert.

Luisa bietet ein großes Interface. War dies von vornherein so geplant oder ergab sich das aus dem Packaging des Gerätes?

Wir haben uns sehr früh für ein 10-Zoll-Touchdisplay entschieden, um dem Anspruch der intuitiven und unkomplizierten Bedienung Rechnung zu tragen. Luisa lässt sich auch aus der Entfernung gut ablesen, Kurven werden komfortabel dargestellt. Auch die zwei Positionierungen des Gerätes unterstützen unterschiedliche Ablesepositionen und Nutzungsszenarien. Zur Ergänzung haben wir noch eine App entwickelt.

Insgesamt ging es uns darum, dem Thema Beatmung durch klares reduziertes Design die Komplexität und den Anwendern die Berührungsängste zu nehmen. Die Technik verschwindet weitestgehend hinter dem großen Screen und Luisa erinnert damit an ein Lifestyle-Produkt.

Welche Relevanz hat Design bei Löwenstein insgesamt – wann werden Sie als Designerin in die Entwicklung einbezogen?

Design und Ergonomie haben bei uns eine hohe Relevanz. Als Inhouse-Designerin bin ich von Anfang an, also bereits in der Konzeptphase, Teil des interdisziplinären Entwicklerteams. So kommen wir zu belastbaren Designkonzepten, die alle Disziplinen berücksichtigen und identitätsstiftend sind.

> Löwenstein Medical Technology ist Teil der Löwenstein Gruppe, die sich seit über 30 Jahren der Medizintechnik widmet. Der in Hamburg ansässige Unternehmensteil ist auf die Fachdisziplinen Schlaf- und Heimbeatmung spezialisiert.
>
> www.loewensteinmedical.com

→ Covid-19 has made us all realise just how important ventilators are – even if Luisa was actually developed for a different kind of usage scenario.

Luisa is a life-sustaining ventilator both for adults who require ventilation and for children with all sorts of different disorders, mainly neuromuscular diseases. Luisa is suitable for use in a home environment as well as in a clinical setting.

Medical devices are long-term projects. When did Luisa's development begin – and which premises were uppermost?

The first step was to establish what expectations patients, doctors, carers and family members have of a new ventilator in this category and what the usage scenarios are like. That was back in 2017. Our approach was to make Luisa as mobile, compact and easy to use as possible. The last aspect is important for safety reasons: if a ventilator is intuitive and straightforward to use, a lot of potential sources of error are eliminated.

Luisa has a large interface. Was that planned right from the start or was it a consequence of the device's packaging?

We decided on a 10-inch touch display at a very early stage as a way to meet the goal of intuitive and straightforward usability. Luisa is easy to read, even from a distance, and the graphs are depicted in a very legible way. Being able to place the device in two different positions also makes it easier to read from wherever you happen to be standing and in different usage scenarios. We also developed an accompanying app.

Our overall goal was to create a clear, minimalist design that takes the complexity out of ventilation and overcomes users' reservations. The technology largely disappears behind the big screen, which is why Luisa resembles a lifestyle product.

How relevant is design at Löwenstein in general – as a designer, when are you brought into the development process?

Design and ergonomics play an extremely relevant role for us. As an in-house designer I'm part of the interdisciplinary development team right from the start, i.e. from the concept stage on. That enables us to come up with viable design concepts that incorporate all the disciplines and create identity.

> Löwenstein Medical Technology is part of the Löwenstein Group, which has been dedicated to medical technology for more than 30 years. The Hamburg-based business unit specialises in sleep and home ventilation.
>
> www.loewensteinmedical.com

SILVER HD 650 ECOPAK DURCHLAUFSIEGELGERÄT / ROTARY SEALER

JURY STATEMENT

Eine schlichte, nutzungsgerechte Gestaltung, die das Thema absolut funktionsbewusst angeht. Sauber gelungen ist die Blechverarbeitung des Gehäuses, die den Dienstleistungscharakter des Gerätes betont.

A simple, fit-for-purpose design that takes a thoroughly function-focused approach. The crisp workmanship of the metal housing underscores the service character of the device.

HERSTELLER / MANUFACTURER
Hawo GmbH
Obrigheim

DESIGN
Inhouse

VERTRIEB / DISTRIBUTOR
Hawo GmbH
Obrigheim

Mehrweginstrumente im Krankenhaus oder in Arzt- und Zahnarztpraxen werden nach der Sterilisation in siegelbaren Beuteln oder Schläuchen verpackt und bis zur Verwendung gelagert. Das automatische Verschließen übernehmen sogenannte Durchlaufsiegelgeräte.

Die mikroprozessorgesteuerte Gerätefamilie mit ihren drei Varianten lässt sich energiesparend betreiben und ressourcenschonend herstellen. Das puristische Design nimmt diese Anforderung auf und verbessert zugleich die Reinigungsfähigkeit der Oberflächen. Die Geräte arbeiten wartungsarm und ermöglichen hohe Durchlaufzahlen.

In hospitals or doctors' and dental practices, reusable instruments are packed in sealable pouches or sleeves after being sterilised and stored until needed. The automatic closing process is performed by devices known as rotary sealers.

Controlled by microprocessors, this family of devices consists of three variants that are energy-efficient to operate and resource-efficient to produce. The purist design reflects these qualities while simultaneously improving the cleanability of the surfaces. The devices require minimal maintenance and deliver a high output.

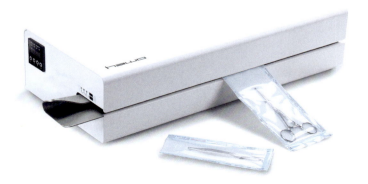

1 → SEITE / PAGE
64, 66

2 → SEITE / PAGE
65, 67

KÜCHE, HAUSHALT, TISCHKULTUR
KITCHEN, HOUSEHOLD, TABLE

SILVER:
1 **KARA 57**
  Systemceram GmbH & Co. KG
  Siershahn

2 **EXCELLENCE LINE**
  V-Zug AG
  Zug
  Schweiz / Switzerland

Kaum ein Wohnbereich ist so perfektioniert, funktional durchdacht und ästhetisch auf so hohem Niveau wie die Küche. Clevere Details, die das Kochen erleichtern, sind ebenso gefragt wie neue Oberflächen oder neue Materialien. Technologische Neuerungen wiederum erleichtern die Arbeit im Haushalt auf überraschende Weise.

There are few areas of the home that exhibit such perfectionism, such well thought-through functionality and such high aesthetic standards as the kitchen. Clever details that make cooking easier are just as much in demand as new finishes or new materials, while technological innovations come up with surprising ways to take the effort out of household chores.

SILVER KARA 57 KÜCHENSPÜLE / KITCHEN SINK

JURY STATEMENT

Eine sehr sauber und ansprechend gestaltete Spüle, die sich durch eine zweite Ebene bedarfsgerecht funktional aufwerten lässt. Interessant: Der Bedienungsknebel für den Ablauf wird außerhalb des Beckens platziert und lässt sich flächenbündig versenken.

A very neatly and attractively designed sink that can be upgraded with a functional second level as needed. It's interesting that the knob for operating the plug is positioned outside the sink and can be pushed down to sit flush with the surface.

HERSTELLER / MANUFACTURER
Systemceram GmbH & Co. KG
Siershahn

DESIGN
IADC GmbH
Ratingen

VERTRIEB / DISTRIBUTOR
Systemceram GmbH & Co. KG
Siershahn

Nicht alle Küchen bieten ausreichend Raum für ein Spülbecken mit angrenzender Abtropffläche. Die Solo-Keramikspüle erhöht deshalb ihre Funktionalität mittels eines cleveren Kniffs: Die vordere und hintere Beckenkante sind leicht nach innen abgeschrägt, was den flexiblen Einsatz verschiedenster Einlegeelemente ermöglicht. So kann beispielsweise die mitgelieferte Einlage aus Aluminium als temporäre Abtropffläche für gespültes Geschirr dienen oder als Abstellfläche, um einen Topf mit Wasser zu befüllen. Nach Gebrauch verschwindet sie platzsparend in der Schublade.

Produziert wird die Spüle in Deutschland, das hygienische Feinsteinzeug ist ein natürlicher Werkstoff, der zu 100 Prozent recyclebar ist.

Not all kitchens are spacious enough for a sink with an adjoining drainer. That's why this solo ceramic sink improves its functionality with a clever trick: the front and back edges slope slightly inwards, permitting versatile usage of various add-ons. The aluminium insert that comes with it, for instance, can be used as a temporary drainer for washed dishes or to stand a saucepan on while filling it with water. After use, the space-saving accessory disappears into the drawer.

Produced in Germany, the sink is made of hygienic porcelain stoneware – a natural material that is 100 percent recyclable.

SILVER EXCELLENCE LINE   KÜCHENGERÄTE / KITCHEN APPLIANCES

JURY STATEMENT

Der kreisförmige Slider erweitert den Touchscreen um ein haptisches Bedienerlebnis, das auf einer analogen Interaktion beruht und die Oberfläche der digitalen Welt emotional auflädt. Das eröffnet eine neue Qualität für die User*innen.

The circular slider enhances the touchscreen by contributing a tactile experience based on analogue interaction, thus adding an emotional touch to the interface with the digital world and introducing a new sensory quality.

HERSTELLER / MANUFACTURER
V-Zug AG
Zug
Schweiz / Switzerland

DESIGN
Milani Design & Consulting AG
Thalwil
Schweiz / Switzerland

VERTRIEB / DISTRIBUTOR
V-Zug Europe BV
Harelbeke
Belgien / Belgium

Mehr als drei Jahre nahm die Entwicklung der Hard- und Software der neuen Einbaugeräte-Linie in Anspruch. Neben der Gestaltung der Gerätefront, die sich nicht vollständig von den Vorgängermodellen ablösen sollte, steckt besonders viel Entwicklungsarbeit im Interface. Es besteht aus einem Touchscreen, der sich mit verschiedenen Hintergrundmotiven bespielen lässt. Teil des Screens ist der Circle Slider, eine in die Glasoberfläche eingefräste Kreismulde, über die sich Einstellungen intuitiv per Fingerbewegung vornehmen lassen. Diese Form der Interaktion reduziert die Komplexität der hinterlegten, digitalen Zubereitungsprozesse und gestaltet das Aufrufen der Programme emotionaler. Zugleich dient der Slider als charakteristisches Markenelement.

It took more than three years to complete the development of the hard- and software for the new line of built-in appliances. Besides the design of the fronts, which was not to depart completely from that of previous models, the development of the interface was particularly demanding. It consists of a touchscreen that can be set to display various background motifs. The Circle Slider is part of the screen: a round depression milled into the surface of the glass that permits intuitive adjustments with a simple movement of the finger. This form of interaction reduces the complexity of the preset digital cooking processes and makes accessing the programs more emotional. At the same time, the slider serves as a characteristic brand element.

TINA KAMMER   **INTERIORPARK., STUTTGART**

»Design steht vor der großen Herausforderung, Dinge so zu entwickeln, dass sie am Ende ihres Lebenszyklus ohne Wertverlust in den Kreislauf zurückgeführt werden können. Design nimmt also eine Kernrolle bei zukunftsfähigen Lösungen ein.«

»Design is facing the major challenge of developing things in such a way that they can be returned to the loop at the end of their life cycle without losing value. Design thus has a core role to play in future-proof solutions.«

Tina Kammer ist gelernte Möbelschreinerin und studierte Innenarchitektur in Mainz. Zunächst arbeitete sie im Londoner Architekturbüro Jestico + Whiles, anschließend betreute sie die Markenarchitektur von Firmen wie BMW oder IBM. Bei der Hugo Boss AG entwickelte sie Ladenkonzepte für den internationalen Markt. Zusammen mit Andrea Herold gründete Tina Kammer 2010 die Online-Plattform InteriorPark., die als Research- und Informationsquelle für nachhaltiges Design dient. Daneben ist das Unternehmen auch als Beratungs- und Planungsstudio für Innenraumkonzepte aktiv.

www.interiorpark.com

Tina Kammer is a qualified cabinetmaker and studied interior design in Mainz. Her first position was at London architectural practice Jestico + Whiles, after which she was responsible for the corporate architecture of firms like BMW and IBM. At Hugo Boss AG, she developed store concepts for the international market. Together with Andrea Herold, Tina Kammer founded InteriorPark. in 2010. The online platform serves as a research and information resource for sustainable design. The studio also provides consulting and planning services for interior concepts.

www.interiorpark.com

1 → SEITE / PAGE
72, 80

2 → SEITE / PAGE
73, 81

3 → SEITE / PAGE
74, 82

4 → SEITE / PAGE
75, 83

5 → SEITE / PAGE
76, 84

6 → SEITE / PAGE
77, 85

7 → SEITE / PAGE
78, 86

INTERIOR
INTERIORS

SILVER:
1 **FLOMO TRAIN SYSTEMS**
Karl Westermann GmbH & Co. KG
Denkendorf

SPECIAL MENTION:
2 **MTD700R WANDERLUST**
Walkolution GmbH
Wiesenbronn

3 **GAR:ASH**
Richard Schmied GmbH
Aalen

4 **X-PRESS**
Bene GmbH
Waidhofen an der Ybbs
Österreich / Austria

5 **ONGO BOARDS**
Ongo GmbH
Stuttgart

6 **AS100 CHAIR**
Howe a/s
Odense
Dänemark / Denmark

7 **AS400 TABLE**
Howe a/s
Odense
Dänemark / Denmark

Ein Stuhl, ein Tisch, ein Bett und ein Regal – was braucht man mehr? Und doch ist das Universum der Möbel immens weit, wandelt sich stetig, erneuert sich und spielt mit Volumina, Materialien, Oberflächen, Farben. Möbeldesign ist eine der populärsten Gestaltungsdisziplinen, die immer wieder überraschende ästhetische und funktionale Novitäten hervorbringt.

A chair, a table, a bed and a shelving unit – what more does anyone need? And yet the world of furniture is truly immense, changes constantly, reinvents itself and plays with volumes, materials, finishes and colours. Furniture design is one of the most popular design disciplines of all and yields an endless stream of surprising aesthetic and functional ideas.

5

| SILVER | FLOMO TRAIN SYSTEMS → SEITE / PAGE 80 | FLEXIBLES ORGANISATIONS-TOOL FLEXIBLE ORGANISATION TOOL |

SPECIAL MENTION GAR:ASH GARDEROBE CLOTHES RACK
→ SEITE / PAGE 82

SPECIAL MENTION — X-PRESS → SEITE / PAGE 83 — ARBEITSTISCH DESK

SPECIAL MENTION

ONGO BOARDS
→ SEITE / PAGE 84

BÜROELEMENTE
OFFICE ELEMENTS

| SPECIAL MENTION | AS100 CHAIR →SEITE / PAGE 85 | KONFERENZSTUHL CONFERENCE CHAIR |

| SPECIAL MENTION | AS400 TABLE → SEITE / PAGE 86 | ARBEITS- / KONFERENZTISCH WORK / CONFERENCE TABLE |

SILVER

FLOMO TRAIN SYSTEMS
FLEXIBLES ORGANISATIONS-TOOL / FLEXIBLE ORGANISATION TOOL

JURY STATEMENT

Das System steckt voller hilfreicher Detaillösungen, dazu gehört zum Beispiel die Integration von Schließfächern. Der robuste Werkstattcharakter unterstreicht die flexible Ad-hoc-Nutzung der einzelnen Module, die auf einer gemeinsamen Typologie basieren.

The system features a wealth of useful details such as the option of integrating lockable compartments. The robust workshop character underscores the flexible ad hoc usability of the individual modules, which are based on a common typology.

HERSTELLER / MANUFACTURER
Karl Westermann GmbH & Co. KG
Denkendorf

DESIGN
wd3 GmbH
Stuttgart
und / and
Res Anima GbR
Dießen a. Ammersee

VERTRIEB / DISTRIBUTOR
wp – products by westermann
Denkendorf

Wo Arbeitsstrukturen immer agiler werden und sich angestammte Arbeitsplätze zu flexiblen Workspaces wandeln, sind adaptive Lösungen für eine entsprechende Möblierung gefragt.

Flomo Train ist ein multifunktionales Organisationssystem, das die unterschiedlichsten Einsatzmöglichkeiten bietet: Mit Whiteboards bestückt, wird der fahrbare Hohlkehlenrahmen zum Präsentationselement, Fachböden machen ihn zum übersichtlichen Stauraum für Ordner und Co.

Mit einer integrierbaren, höhenverstellbaren Tischplatte lässt sich der mobile Rahmen sogar zu einem optisch und akustisch abgeschirmten Mikroarbeitsplatz umgestalten – die mobile Ein-Personen-Schreibstube ist geboren.

Wherever work structures are becoming increasingly agile and traditional workplaces are turning into flexible workspaces, there is a need for adaptive solutions that can provide corresponding furnishings.

Flomo Train is a multifunctional organisation system designed for a wide range of uses: equipped with whiteboards, the wheeled concave frame becomes a presentation element, while the addition of shelves creates storage space for files and other items.

The integration of a height-adjustable tabletop even transforms the mobile frame into a micro-workstation with screening and acoustic benefits – the mobile one-person writing room is born.

SPECIAL MENTION — MTD700R WANDERLUST — MOBILES LAUFBAND MIT ARBEITSTISCH / MOBILE TREADMILL WITH DESK

JURY STATEMENT

Dass Bewegung den Denkapparat anregt und so bessere Ideen entstehen, dürfte sich schon herumgesprochen haben. Das Laufband setzt diese Erkenntnis nun in einer für das Büro kompatiblen Form um und ergänzt die Arbeitswelt um ein weiteres, individuell nutzbares Angebot. Profis sollen sogar Laufen und Tippen kombinieren können.

It's no secret that exercise stimulates the mind and helps it come up with better ideas as a result. The treadmill translates this knowledge into a form that's compatible with the office and enhances the world of work with the addition of an offering that meets a variety of individual needs. Real pros are even said to be able to walk and type at the same time.

HERSTELLER/MANUFACTURER
Walkolution GmbH
Wiesenbronn

DESIGN
Inhouse

VERTRIEB/DISTRIBUTOR
Walkolution GmbH
Wiesenbronn

Viele Menschen verbringen ihre Arbeits- und Lernzeiten nahezu ausschließlich im Sitzen – das kann unter Umständen fatale Auswirkungen auf die Gesundheit und damit die Lebensqualität haben. Ergonomische Alternativen zum statischen Sitzen gibt es einige, aber das mobile Laufband mit integriertem Arbeitstisch geht noch einen Schritt weiter. Das motorlose, wartungsfreie Laufband ermöglicht Arbeiten und Lernen mit gleichzeitigem Gehen und integriert so aktive Bewegung in den Arbeitsalltag. Pausen können jederzeit eingelegt werden, eine Stehhilfe erlaubt entspanntes Zurücklehnen bei dann blockiertem Band. Dank seiner Kompaktheit und der fahrbaren Rollen sind unterschiedlichste Nutzungen möglich – als Workspace im Büro oder Arbeitsplatz im Homeoffice.

Many people spend almost their entire work or study time sitting down – which can have disastrous effects on their health and therefore seriously impact their quality of life. While various ergonomic alternatives to static sitting are already available, the mobile treadmill with integrated desk goes one step further. The motorless, maintenance-free treadmill makes it possible to combine working and studying with walking, thereby integrating active movement into everyday working life. The user can take a break whenever they want by leaning back on a standing aid, which blocks the treadmill. Thanks to its compactness and casters, it can be used in a variety of ways – as a workspace at the office or a workstation at home.

SPECIAL MENTION   GAR:ASH   GARDEROBE
                                        CLOTHES RACK

> **JURY STATEMENT**
>
> Hier wurde ein Alltagsthema charmant neu interpretiert, sehr reduziert und doch eigenständig umgesetzt. Dank eines konstruktiv durchdachten Kniffs lässt sich die Garderobe schraubenlos aufbauen und stabilisiert sich selbst. Die Umsetzung in Holz zeigt ein hohes handwerkliches Niveau.
>
> A charming reinterpretation of an everyday object, implemented in a very minimalist yet original way. Thanks to an ingenious trick, the construction can be put together without screws and stabilises itself. Its implementation in wood exhibits a high standard of craftsmanship.

HERSTELLER / MANUFACTURER
Richard Schmied GmbH
Aalen

DESIGN
Valentin Schmied
Aalen

VERTRIEB / DISTRIBUTOR
Richard Schmied GmbH
Aalen

Immer wieder ein Thema zu Hause: Wohin mit Jacken, Mänteln, Taschen und Schuhen des täglichen Gebrauchs? Abhilfe verspricht hier die flexible, aus unterschiedlichen Rahmen ineinandergesteckte Garderobe aus Eschenholz. Ein oder zwei Ablageböden bieten Platz für Schuhe und Utensilien, die oberen Rahmenleisten eignen sich zum Hängen von Kleidung. Der Clou dabei: Je mehr auf der Garderobe lastet, desto stabiler wird sie, da sich die Rahmen durch die auftretende Spannung fest miteinander verbinden.

Mittels einer optional erhältlichen, verschiebbaren Holzbox und der Wahl zwischen unterschiedlichen Oberflächen und Farbausführungen lässt sich die Garderobe verschiedenen Wohnumfeldern und individuellen Vorlieben anpassen.

It's a problem that comes up again and again in most homes: where to put the jackets, coats, bags and shoes that we use on a daily basis? Put together out of various frames, this flexible ash coat rack provides a remedy. One or two shelf panels provide space for shoes and accessories, the upper bars of the frame are ideal for hanging clothes. And best of all: the more weight the rack has to support, the more stable it is – the resulting tension joins the frames firmly together.

Thanks to an optional sliding wooden box and a choice of two different finishes and colours, the clothes rack can be adapted to various interior settings and individual preferences.

| SPECIAL MENTION | X-PRESS | ARBEITSTISCH / DESK |

JURY STATEMENT

Der Tisch passt ideal in eine Zeit der Interims-Arbeitsplätze. Er fügt sich mit seiner geradlinigen Gestaltung in jedes Interior ein und lässt sich bei Nichtgebrauch gut verstauen. Außerdem löst er auf einfache Weise nutzungsrelevante Aspekte wie die Höhenverstellung und das Kabelmanagement mittels eines Packnetzes an der Unterseite.

This desk is ideal for a time when interim work arrangements are commonplace. Thanks to its straight-lined design, it blends in with any interior and is easy to store when not in use. It also provides simple solutions for relevant aspects like height adjustment or cable management, the latter in the form of a mesh pocket on the underside of the tabletop.

HERSTELLER / MANUFACTURER
Bene GmbH
Waidhofen an der Ybbs
Österreich / Austria

DESIGN
Inhouse
Christian Horner

VERTRIEB / DISTRIBUTOR
Bene GmbH
München / Munich

Unser Arbeitsalltag befindet sich in einem tiefgreifenden Wandel: Arbeitszeiten werden flexibler, Arbeitsformen gestalten sich komplexer. Arbeit wird zunehmend unabhängiger von einem festen Standort. Die Corona-Pandemie hat diese Entwicklung noch verstärkt: Plötzlich fanden sich viele Menschen im Homeoffice wieder und benötigten neue Organisationsstrukturen.

Der Arbeitstisch dient nicht nur als individueller Workspace in agilen Umgebungen, sondern bietet auch im heimischen Arbeits- oder Schlafzimmer eine solide Grundlage für jedes Homeoffice. Die Höhe kann über drei Stufen an die eigenen Bedürfnisse angepasst werden. Nach getaner Arbeit lässt sich der Tisch zusammenklappen und platzsparend verstauen.

Our day-to-day working lives are undergoing profound change: working hours are becoming more flexible, the ways of working more complex. Work is becoming increasingly independent of a fixed location. The corona pandemic intensified this development: many people suddenly found themselves working from home and needed new organisation structures.

Besides serving as an individual work space in agile settings, the table can also be used in the living room or bedroom and provides a sound basis for any home office. Thanks to three different settings, the height can be adjusted to individual needs. And when work is done for the day, the desk is simply folded up for easy storage.

SPECIAL MENTION ONGO BOARDS BÜROELEMENTE / OFFICE ELEMENTS

JURY STATEMENT

Das modulare System besticht durch seine einfache Formensprache und die einfache Anpassbarkeit an stetig wechselnde Arbeitsstrukturen. Sehr schön gelöst ist das magnetische Verbindungsprinzip und die multiple Nutzung einzelner Elemente. So kann der Hocker auch die Funktion des Board-Stabilisators übernehmen.

The modular system is impressive for its simple design language and the ease with which it can adapt to constantly changing work structures. The magnetic connection principle and multiple uses for individual elements are compelling: the stool, for instance, can double as a board stabiliser.

HERSTELLER / MANUFACTURER
Ongo GmbH
Stuttgart

DESIGN
UP Designstudio GmbH & Co. KG
Stuttgart

VERTRIEB / DISTRIBUTOR
Ongo GmbH
Stuttgart

Arbeit im Office-Alltag gestaltet sich zunehmend kollaborativer und agiler – das erfordert flexible Strukturen mit modularen, frei konfigurierbaren Bausteinen.

Drei verschiedene Board-Varianten ergänzen das beliebig erweiterbare Pop-Up-Office-Konzept des Herstellers. Die Click Boards haben einen Kern aus Wellkarton und sind auf einer Seite mit Whiteboardfolie, auf der anderen mit einem akustisch wirksamen, recycelten PET-Vlies kaschiert. Mittels Magnetverbindung lassen sich die federleichten Boards völlig variabel kombinieren.

Im Gegensatz dazu sind die Team Boards fahrbar und können auf ihrem Fuß bis zu sechs Click Boards mitführen. Ihre Trägerplatte besteht aus Multiplex. In der Ausführung als Monitor Board verbirgt die PET-Vliesauflage einen Kabelkanal, eine Mehrfachsteckdose ist ebenfalls integriert.

Everyday office work is becoming increasingly collaborative and agile – and that calls for flexible structures with modular, freely configurable components.

Three different board versions have now been added to the manufacturer's infinitely extendable pop-up office concept. The Click Boards have a corrugated cardboard core and are covered with whiteboard foil on one side and sound-absorbing, recycled PET felt on the other. Thanks to magnetic connectors, the featherweight boards can be used to create completely variable combinations.

By contrast, the Team Boards are mobile and can carry up to six Click Boards on their base, which is made of multiplex. The Monitor Board version has concealed cable channelling under the PET felt, as well as an integrated multiple power socket.

SPECIAL MENTION — AS100 CHAIR

KONFERENZSTUHL / CONFERENCE CHAIR

JURY STATEMENT

Das Stapeln mal anders anzugehen, ist eine prima Idee. Dank des speziell gestalteten Fußkreuzes und der Klapp-Sitzschale können mehrere Stühle einfach ineinandergeschoben werden und gelangen so schnell zum nächsten Einsatzort.

Taking a whole new approach to stacking is an excellent idea. Thanks to the specially designed four-star base and lift-up shell, several chairs can simply be pushed together and quickly moved to wherever they're needed next.

HERSTELLER/MANUFACTURER
Howe a/s
Odense
Dänemark/Denmark

DESIGN
Störiko Product Design GmbH
Hamburg

VERTRIEB/DISTRIBUTOR
Howe a/s
Odense
Dänemark/Denmark

Der fahrbare Drehstuhl orientiert sich an den aktuellen Ansprüchen flexibler Settings und agiler Prozesse in Arbeits- und Lernumgebungen. Mit einem Gewicht von knapp zwölf Kilogramm ist er eher ein Leichtgewicht. Ein fahrbares Fußkreuz mit Doppelrollen nimmt die Sitzschale aus Buchenholz auf – wahlweise ohne oder mit Polsterung. Das patentierte Stapelsystem erlaubt ein einfaches Manövrieren mehrerer Stühle im Verbund an den vorgesehenen Ort oder ein platzsparendes Verstauen bei Nichtgebrauch. Dazu wird die Sitzfläche per Gasdruckhebel leicht schräg gestellt und unter die Sitzfläche des Vorgängers geschoben. Eine Magnetfixierung hält die einzelnen Stühle aufgereiht während des Schiebens zusammen.

The mobile swivel chair is geared to the current demand for flexible settings and agile processes in working and learning environments. Weighing in at not even 12 kilograms, it's one of the lighter representatives of its category. The beech shell – available with or without upholstery – is supported by a wheeled four-star base with double casters. The patented horizontal stacking system makes it easy to manoeuvre several chairs at once and take them wherever they're needed, as well as saving storage space when they're not in use. The seat is simply tilted slightly using the gas lever and pushed under the seat of the chair in front. A magnetic fixing keeps the individual chairs in a neat line as they're pushed along.

SPECIAL MENTION

AS400 TABLE

ARBEITS-/KONFERENZTISCH
WORK/CONFERENCE TABLE

> **JURY STATEMENT**
>
> Ein absolut zeitgemäßes Konzept, in dem mehr Ideen stecken als der erste Blick offenbart. Der sehr nutzungsvariabel gedachte Tisch lässt sich dank des zunächst dekorativ anmutenden Kreisausschnittes zu beliebigen Arrangements addieren und damit verschiedensten Situationen anpassen – oder mit geklappter Platte eng verstauen.
>
> A thoroughly contemporary concept full of more ideas than it might first seem. Designed for a wide variety of uses, the table's concave recess – which initially seems like a purely decorative touch – means it can be combined to create any conceivable arrangement and adapted to all sorts of different situations. When the top is folded up, the tables can be placed close together to save valuable storage space.

Tische, die im Büroalltag unterschiedlichen Raumanforderungen genügen müssen, sind im Idealfall leicht und klappbar, um einen mühelosen Transport und ein platzsparendes Verstauen zu ermöglichen. Der Arbeitstisch aus der dänischen AS-Serie geht noch einen Schritt weiter: Er besitzt ein fahrbares Untergestell mit vier Rollen, was das Manövrieren an unterschiedliche Standorte sehr leicht macht. Zusammengeklappt erlaubt ein Griff das Tragen über Treppen und andere Hindernisse.

Eine konkave Aussparung, genau an die Rundung eines zweiten Tisches angepasst, erlaubt das freie Kombinieren zu variablen Tischlandschaften.

Ideally, tables that have to meet different space needs in day-to-day office life are light and foldable so as to permit effortless transport and space-saving storage. The table from the Danish AS series goes one step further: it has a mobile base with four double casters, making it extremely easy to manoeuvre for deployment elsewhere. When the tabletop is flipped up, a handle on the underside enables the user to negotiate stairs and other obstacles while carrying it.

A concave recess that forms an exact fit with the rounded edge of a second table permits infinite combinations and variable setups.

HERSTELLER/MANUFACTURER
Howe a/s
Odense
Dänemark/Denmark

DESIGN
Störiko Product Design GmbH
Hamburg

VERTRIEB/DISTRIBUTOR
Howe a/s
Odense
Dänemark/Denmark

86
87

1 → SEITE / PAGE
90–95

2 → SEITE / PAGE
96–101

3 → SEITE / PAGE
102, 106

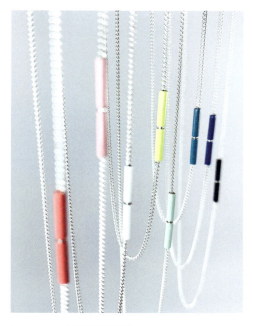

4 → SEITE / PAGE
103, 107

5 → SEITE / PAGE
104, 108

LIFESTYLE, ACCESSOIRES
LIFESTYLE, ACCESSORIES

1 **GOLD:**
FLOYD CABIN, FLOYD CHECK-IN, FLOYD TRUNK
Floyd GmbH
München / Munich

2 **MAX BILL MEGA SOLAR**
Uhrenfabrik
Junghans GmbH & Co. KG
Schramberg

3 **SILVER:**
CLAVIUS
Botta-Design
Königstein

4 **LINES**
bKing Design
Zwiesel

5 **SPECIAL MENTION:**
BELVEDERE
Robbe & Berking Silbermanufaktur seit 1874 GmbH & Co. KG
Flensburg

Sich mit positiven, sinnlich anregenden oder funktional durchdachten Dingen zu umgeben, macht den Alltag einfacher, facettenreich und inspirierend. Das gilt insbesondere für die kleinen Produkte, die uns durch den ganzen Tag begleiten, uns in bestimmten Situationen unterstützen, das Leben erleichtern oder ganz einfach zur Freude gereichen.

Surrounding oneself with positive things that appeal to the senses or are equipped with clever functions makes everyday life easier, more varied and more inspiring. That particularly applies to little products that accompany us throughout the day, provide support in certain situations, make life easier or simply give us pleasure.

GOLD

FLOYD CABIN,
FLOYD CHECK-IN,
FLOYD TRUNK

HARTSCHALENKOFFER
HARD SHELL SUITCASES

LIFESTYLE, ACCESSOIRES
LIFESTYLE, ACCESSORIES

IN, FOCUS GOLD HART ALENKOFFER

GOLD

FLOYD CABIN, FLOYD CHECK-IN, FLOYD TRUNK
HARTSCHALENKOFFER
HARD SHELL SUITCASES

JURY STATEMENT

Ein ausgesprochen wertiges und komplett durchgestaltetes Produkt. Die Polyurethan-Rollen bewegen sich sicher auf allen Böden, sind leise und lösen endlich das Problem der lästigen Rollkoffer-Akustik. Die mitgelieferte Hülle schützt vor Regen und hartem Handling bei der Verladung. Sehr schön ist die stabile Innenausstattung.

An extremely high-quality product that has been designed right down to the last detail. The polyurethane wheels run smoothly on any kind of surface; they are quiet and finally solve the annoying problem of the noise level usually associated with trolley cases. The accompanying cover provides protection from rain and rough handling when the suitcases are loaded onto the plane. The sturdy interior compartments are very appealing.

HERSTELLER/MANUFACTURER
Floyd GmbH
München/Munich

DESIGN
Panoorama
München/Munich

VERTRIEB/DISTRIBUTOR
Floyd GmbH
München/Munich

Wer reist, braucht einen Koffer – aber den richtigen. Für alle, die den lässigen Style der kalifornischen Skateboard-Kultur der 1970er-Jahre zelebrieren, ist diese Kofferserie gedacht. Alle drei Modelle – 41, 61 oder 82 Liter groß – fahren auf bunten Skateboard-Rollen. Das geschieht akustisch erfreulich leise und zugleich wendig, weil jede Rolle um 360 Grad drehbar ist. Die Koffer bestehen aus Polycarbonat, der Aluminiumrahmen sorgt zusammen mit dem Klickverschluss für passgenaues Schließen. Die Metalliclackierung der Schalen ist in neun Retro-Farben mit schillernden Namen wie Sunset Orange oder Magic Purple zu haben, auch die Rollen stehen in unterschiedlichen Transparenttönen bereit. Dank der vier Rollenpaare kann der Koffer sogar im Stehen geöffnet werden. Die orangefarbene Innenseparierung verhindert dabei, dass sich der Inhalt des Koffers selbstständig macht.

If you travel, you need a suitcase – but the right one. This series is meant for fans of the casual style cultivated by California's 1970s skateboarding culture. All three models – with a volume of 41, 61 or 82 litres – run on brightly coloured skateboard wheels that swivel a full 360 degrees, making the suitcases pleasantly quiet and extremely manoeuvrable. The polycarbonate shells have an aluminium frame with a click-shut mechanism for perfect closure. The metallic finish of the shells comes in nine retro colours with flamboyant names like Sunset Orange or Magic Purple, and the wheels are also available in various transparent hues. Thanks to the four sets of wheels, the case can even be opened in an upright position. The orange interior organiser ensures the contents stay neatly in place.

JULIAN GERBLINGER DESIGNER,
PANOORAMA DESIGNBÜRO

»Wir wollten einen coolen
Koffer entwickeln,
der viel besser rollt als andere.«

»We wanted to develop a cool case
that rolls a lot better than others.«

links / left: Christian Wessolowski
rechts / right: Julian Gerblinger

JULIAN GERBLINGER **DESIGNER, PANOORAMA DESIGNBÜRO**

→ **Eine grundsätzliche Frage gleich mal vorweg: Wieso braucht die Welt eigentlich noch mehr Rollkoffer?**
Ganz einfach. Weil das Bessere immer das Alte verdrängt. Einen Koffer wie den Floyd gab es bislang noch nicht. Natürlich existiert eine unglaubliche Zahl an Rollkoffern, aber die allermeisten sind qualitativ einfach miserabel. Die Rollen sind schlecht, es klappert und rumpelt. Beim Floyd hingegen ist jede Rolle kugelgelagert. Das Feedback, das wir und der Hersteller regelmäßig bekommen, macht unglaublich viel Spaß und zeigt, dass der Koffer tatsächlich gebraucht wird.

Mit welchen Intentionen sind Sie an den Start gegangen?
Die Initiatoren hinter Floyd, Bernd Georgi und Horst Kern, wollten einen coolen Koffer entwickeln, der viel besser rollt als andere und obendrein auch praktischer und haltbarer ist. Der kreative Kopf Bernd Georgi hatte bei unserem ersten Termin einen Koffer aus den 1970er-Jahren auf ein Skateboard aus seiner Sammlung gestellt. Das war das Briefing. Wir haben daraufhin ausgiebig alte Bildbände mit Skatern und Surfern gewälzt. Das Projekt hat also gleich mit unglaublich viel Spaß und Herzblut begonnen.

Wann kamen die Skateboard-Rollen dazu?
Ganz am Anfang, sie waren der eigentliche Kern der Idee. Die weitere Entwicklung war nicht ganz so einfach. Es mussten Achsen konstruiert und Materialien sowie Querschnitte getestet werden, um beispielsweise das Gewicht im Normwert zu halten. Letztendlich stehen die Rollen in Material und Farbe echten Skateboard-Rollen nicht nach. Mit dem eigens angefertigten Schraubenschlüssel kann man einfach und schnell die mittlerweile neun verschiedenfarbigen Rollensets tauschen.

Welche Rolle spielte die Innenausstattung für die Konzeption?
Der Koffer sollte positiver und hochwertiger rüberkommen als all die bekannten Koffer mit ihrem langweiligen, meist schwarzen Innenleben. Deshalb haben wir uns für die lebensbejahende Farbe Orange entschieden, die nicht nur unsere signature-Farbe ist, sondern auch wie keine andere Farbe für den Zeitgeist der 1970er steht. Außerdem wollten wir Oeko-Tex-Material mit sattem Griff einsetzen und das Friseurkittel-Feeling vermeiden, das man bei vielen anderen Marken antrifft. Dass beide Fächer mit Reißverschlüssen verschließbar sind, ergab sich schon allein aus dem Umstand, dass man den Floyd ja stehend öffnen kann und dabei irgendwelche Dinge rausfallen können.

> Panoorama wurde 2014 von Christian Wessolowski und Julian Gerblinger in München gegründet. Das Büro widmet sich der Gestaltung von Messeauftritten, Ausstellungen und Produkten, die auch schon mal – wie bei einer Servopresse – Hausgröße haben können.
> Floyd produziert seit 1996 Accessoires, Koffer und andere Gepäckbehältnisse für große Marken. Mit dem gleichnamigen Rollkoffer greift Floyd den Spirit und Style der 1970er-Skateboard-Pioniere auf, zu denen sich auch die beiden Gründer zählen.
>
> www.panoorama.de
> www.floyd.one

→ **Let me start off by asking you a fundamental question: why does the world actually need any more trolley cases?**
It's simple: because better is always the enemy of the old. There has never been a suitcase like Floyd before. It's true that there are an incredible number of trolley cases on the market, but the vast majority are really lousy when it comes to quality. The wheels are no good, so they clatter and rumble. Whereas every one of Floyd's wheels has a ball bearing. The feedback that we and the manufacturer regularly get is great fun and shows that there really is a need for the case.

What were your intentions when you started out?
The initiators behind Floyd, Bernd Georgi and Horst Kern, wanted to develop a cool case that rolls a lot better than others and is more practical and hardwearing as well. At our first meeting the creative behind the idea, Bernd Georgi, stood a 1970s suitcase on a skateboard from his collection. That was our briefing. After that, we spent ages poring over old books of photos of skaters and surfers. So the project was great fun and we put our heart and soul into it right from the start.

At what point did the skateboard wheels come into it?
Right at the outset, they were actually the core of the idea. But moving forward, the development was by no means easy. We had to design axles and test both materials and cross-sections, e.g. to make sure we kept within the standard weight. At the end of the day, the wheels are every bit as good as real skateboard wheels in terms of material and colour. And with the custom-made wrench, it's quick and easy to replace them – the wheel sets are now available in nine different colours.

What role did the interior compartments play in the concept?
We wanted the case to come across as more positive and better quality than all the familiar alternatives with their boring, usually black interiors. That's why we decided on orange; besides being very optimistic, it's also our signature colour and second to none when it comes to capturing the spirit of the 1970s. We also wanted to use an Oeko-Tex material with a rich texture and avoid the hairdressing cape feel you encounter with so many other brands. The fact that both compartments are equipped with zips was only logical given that you can open Floyd while it's standing upright: we wanted to avoid the risk of anything falling out.

> Panoorama was founded in Munich by Christian Wessolowski and Julian Gerblinger in 2014. The firm designs trade show booths, exhibitions and products, some of which – like a servo press, for instance – can be as big as a house.
> Floyd has been producing accessories, suitcases and other luggage for major brands since 1996. With its trolley case of the same name, Floyd is echoing the spirit and style of the pioneering 1970s skateboard culture, which the two founders were part of.
>
> www.panoorama.de
> www.floyd.one

GOLD | MAX BILL MEGA SOLAR | ARMBANDUHR WRISTWATCH

ARM-
BANDUHR

LIFESTYLE, ACCESSOIRES
LIFESTYLE, ACCESSORIES

MAX BILL
MEGA
SOLAR
FOCUS
GOLD

GOLD — MAX BILL MEGA SOLAR — ARMBANDUHR / WRISTWATCH

JURY STATEMENT

Die Uhr beweist, dass klassische Designentwürfe bis heute Bestand haben können und technisch in die Gegenwart übersetzbar sind. Besonders hervorzuheben ist das geringe Gewicht der Uhr und die geschickte, nicht sichtbare Einbindung der solaren Energieerzeugung.

The watch not only proves that classic designs can withstand the test of time but that they can be translated into the present technologically as well. The lightness of the watch and the clever, invisible integration of the technology that generates its solar energy deserve special mention.

Bereits 1962 entwarf Max Bill diese minimalistische Armbanduhr, die mittlerweile zum Designklassiker avanciert ist. Im Inneren arbeitet inzwischen modernste Technologie: Die exakte Zeitermittlung übernimmt ein photovoltaisch mit Energie versorgtes Multifrequenz-Funkmodul. Die Solarzelle befindet sich unsichtbar unter dem grauen, aber lichtdurchlässigen Ziffernblatt, sie speist einen integrierten Speicher, der eine sechsmonatige Gangreserve gewährleistet. Für den täglichen Normalbetrieb genügt es, die Uhr über zwei Minuten im direkten Sonnenlicht zu platzieren; der Ladezustand des Speichers lässt sich über die Position des Sekundenzeigers anzeigen. Lediglich neun Millimeter hoch, bleibt das Gehäuse sehr schlank und besteht, wie auch das Armband, aus Titan. Damit ist es sehr leicht, robust und hautfreundlich.

This minimalist watch was created by Max Bill back in 1962 and rose to become a design classic. Meanwhile, there is state-of-the-art technology inside the case: the precise time is determined by a multi-frequency radio-controlled module powered by photovoltaic energy. An integrated power reservoir is supplied with energy by an invisible solar cell beneath the grey but translucent dial and guarantees a six-month power reserve. Exposing the watch to direct sunlight for two minutes is sufficient for normal daily use; the remaining power reserve is indicated via the position of the second hand. The extremely slender case is just nine millimetres high and, like the strap, is made of titanium. As a result, the watch is extremely light, robust and skin-friendly.

HERSTELLER/MANUFACTURER
Uhrenfabrik
Junghans GmbH & Co. KG
Schramberg

DESIGN
Inhouse

VERTRIEB/DISTRIBUTOR
Uhrenfabrik
Junghans GmbH & Co. KG
Schramberg

MATTHIAS STOTZ GESCHÄFTSFÜHRER, UHRENFABRIK JUNGHANS GMBH & CO. KG

»Nur durch einen integrativen Prozess von Konstruktion und Design lassen sich derart kompromisslose Produkte realisieren.«

»An integrative process that combines engineering and design is the only way to create such an uncompromising product as this.«

MATTHIAS STOTZ — MANAGING DIRECTOR, UHRENFABRIK JUNGHANS GMBH & CO. KG

→ **Die prämierte Uhr baut auf einem klassischen Entwurf auf – was sprach für die technische Modernisierung?**
Als traditioneller Uhrenhersteller spielt für uns Präzision seit jeher eine große Rolle. Die Funkuhr bietet viele Vorteile in Regionen mit Funkempfang. Unser neu entwickeltes Funkwerk ermöglicht nun auch den Komfort, an jedem Ort die Zeit über eine App zu synchronisieren. Somit kann das ästhetische Design, gepaart mit der neuesten Technologie, überall genutzt werden. Für uns vereint die Uhr die Kernkompetenzen von Junghans: gutes Design und absolute Präzision.

Wie gut ließ sich diese Modernisierung mit dem Original vereinbaren?
Sehr gut, da wir bereits beim Entwicklungsstart des Uhrwerkes die Kompatibilität mit unserem Design in den Fokus gestellt haben. Auch der Einsatz des besonders hautfreundlichen Materials Titan passt hier gut, denn es bietet einen hohen Tragekomfort – ganz im Sinne von Max Bill, für den die Verbindung von Gebrauchswert und Anmutung eine große Rolle spielte. Bill betrachtete seine Werke zudem als Gestaltung der Umwelt, dies greifen wir durch den Antrieb mit Solarenergie auf, der Verzicht auf Batterien schont die Umwelt.

Junghans setzt stark auf technische Kompetenz in Sachen Funkuhr. Wie arbeiten Entwicklung und Design zusammen?
Da wir eigene Abteilungen für Werkentwicklung, Design und Konstruktion im Haus haben, findet die Abstimmung sehr frühzeitig statt. Nur durch diesen integrativen Prozess lassen sich derart kompromisslose Produkte realisieren.

Braucht es für das Uhrendesign spezifische Kompetenzen?
Definitiv, mehr noch als bei anderen Produkten. Ein Verständnis für kleinste Dimensionen und viel Liebe zum Detail, wenn nicht gar Akribie, sind notwendig. Im Fall einer Traditionsmarke wie Junghans muss ein*e Designer*in in der Lage sein, Klassiker zu pflegen, aber auch behutsam weiterzuentwickeln. Es ist wichtig, dass Design und Marke im Einklang stehen.

Sie produzieren im süddeutschen Hochlohnland – warum?
Wir haben uns auf authentische Produkte Made in Germany spezialisiert und produzieren seit 160 Jahren am Standort Schramberg. Wir fertigen heute zwar deutlich weniger Uhren als etwa 1903, als wir die größte Uhrenfabrik der Welt waren. Dafür ist heute die Detailarbeit viel entscheidender. Die Käufer*innen schätzen Marken mit echten Werten, und hier gehört neben einem guten Design und qualitativ hochwertigen Produkten auch die Verbundenheit zum Standort dazu.

1861 in Schramberg im Schwarzwald gegründet, entwickelte sich Junghans um die Jahrhundertwende zum damals weltweit führenden Uhrenhersteller. Durch technische Innovationen, wie beispielsweise die erste funkgesteuerte Armbanduhr und Neuinterpretationen historischer Klassiker, setzt das Unternehmen bis heute internationale Standards in der Uhrenherstellung.

www.junghans.de

→ **The award-winning watch is based on a classic design – what were the arguments in favour of modernising the technology?**
As a traditional watchmaker, precision has always played a key role for us. The radio-controlled watch offers a lot of benefits in regions with radio reception. Now our newly developed radio-controlled movement provides the added convenience of being able to synchronise the time via an app wherever you happen to be. As a result the beautiful design, paired with state-of-the-art technology, can be used anywhere. For us, the watch combines the core competencies of Junghans: good design and absolute precision.

How compatible was this modernisation with the original?
It was no problem at all, because from the moment we started developing the movement we focused on its compatibility with our design. Using titanium, which is an extremely skin-friendly material, was also a good move because it makes the watch very comfortable to wear – and that's very much in keeping with Max Bill's philosophy: for him, the combination of utility and beauty played a major role. Bill also regarded his works as a way of shaping the world around us, and we pick up on that by powering the watch with solar energy: dispensing with batteries is good for the environment.

Junghans relies heavily on technical competence when it comes to radio-controlled watches. How do development and design work together?
Because we have our own in-house departments for movement development, design and engineering, coordination begins at a very early stage. This integrative process is the only way to create such an uncompromising product as this.

Does designing watches call for specific competencies?
Definitely, even more so than with other products. You need an understanding of the tiniest dimensions as well as a passion for detail and painstaking precision. A designer who works for a brand with such a long tradition as Junghans needs to be able to cultivate classics while ensuring their ongoing but gentle evolution. It's important for there to be a good fit between the design and the brand.

You produce in southern Germany, which is known as a high-wage region – why?
We specialise in authentic products made in Germany and have been based at our site in Schramberg for 160 years. Although we make far fewer watches now than we used to in, say, 1903, when we were the biggest watch factory in the world, the detailing plays a much more crucial role nowadays. Customers appreciate brands with genuine values, and besides a good design and top-quality products that includes loyalty to your location as well.

Founded in the Black Forest town of Schramberg in 1861, Junghans had risen to become the world's leading watchmaker by around the turn of the century. Thanks to technical innovations such as the first radio-controlled watch and reinterpretations of historic classics, the company continues to set international benchmarks in the watchmaking industry to this day.

www.junghans.de

SILVER CLAVIUS ARMBANDUHR
WRISTWATCH
→ SEITE / PAGE
106

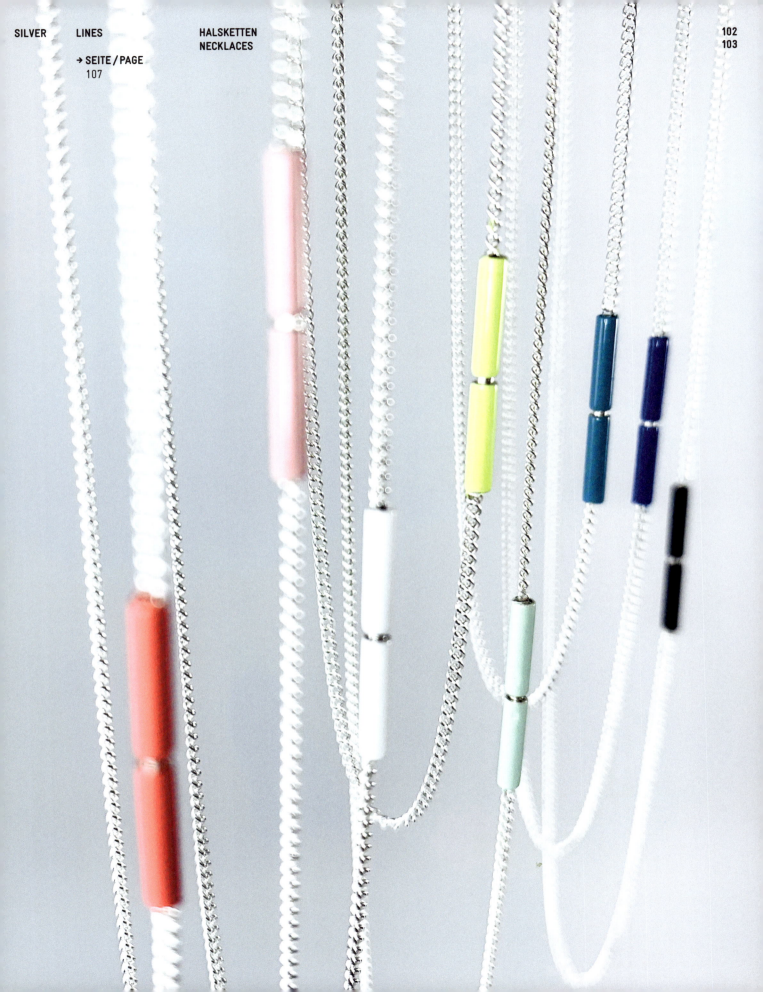

SPECIAL MENTION | **BELVEDERE** → SEITE / PAGE 108 | **BARKOLLEKTION BAR COLLECTION**

SILVER | CLAVIUS | ARMBANDUHR / WRISTWATCH

JURY STATEMENT

Trotz ihrer Größe bietet die Uhr einen überraschenden Tragekomfort. Sie ist sehr sauber durchgestaltet, alle Details stimmen, das Zifferblatt mit der analogen Zeitanzeige ist ganz eigenständig konzipiert.

Despite its size, the watch is surprisingly comfortable to wear. Every detail of this crisp design is perfect, and the dial with its analogue display is highly original.

HERSTELLER / MANUFACTURER
Botta-Design
Königstein

DESIGN
Inhouse

VERTRIEB / DISTRIBUTOR
Botta-Design
Königstein

Obwohl auf dem schwarzen Zifferblatt mit 12-Stunden-Skalierung die klassischen drei Zeiger ihre Arbeit verrichten, hinterlässt die Zeitanzeige den Eindruck des Digitalen: Von Stunden- und Minutenzeiger sind lediglich die Spitzen zu sehen, die aus dem Dunkel hervorleuchten. Der Sekundenzeiger umrundet das Uhrzentrum, taucht jede Sekunde auf, um dann wieder zu verschwinden – ein rhythmisch oszillierender Taktgeber.

Trotz der digitalen Anmutung arbeitet im Inneren des Edelstahlgehäuses ein Schweizer Automatikwerk. Der Uhrenboden gibt den Blick auf ebendieses Uhrwerk frei, er besteht, wie das doppelt gewölbte Uhrglas auch, aus Saphirglas.

Although the black 12-hour dial is actually equipped with the classic three hands, there's a digital quality to the time display all the same: all that's visible of the hour and minute hands are the very tips, glowing against the dark face. The second hand circles the centre of the watch, coming into view every second only to disappear again – a rhythmically oscillating metronome.

Despite this digital aura, the stainless steel case contains a Swiss automatic movement that is visible through the base of the timepiece, which – like the double-curved watch glass – is made of sapphire crystal.

SILVER LINES — HALSKETTEN / NECKLACES

JURY STATEMENT

Hier wird das, was man normalerweise zwangsläufig hinnehmen muss, der Verschluss, zu einem zusätzlichen Schmuckelement der Kette. Obendrein noch farbig akzentuiert, ist das eine feine, subtile Idee.

This chain transforms something that is normally a »necessary evil« – the clasp – into an additional decorative element that contributes an attractive colour accent as well. A subtle and sophisticated idea.

Was andere Halsketten diskret verstecken, wird hier zum Blickfang: der Kettenverschluss. Die filigranen, in drei Längen erhältlichen Silberketten enden in einem farbig gefassten Bajonettverschluss, der sich selbst zum Statement erhebt. Die Drehmechanik ermöglicht es, ganz unkompliziert auch mehrere Ketten direkt miteinander zu verbinden und dabei verschiedene Kettenlängen sowie einen ganz persönlichen, individuellen Farbmix zu kreieren.

In this case, an element that other necklaces do their best to conceal is turned into an eye-catcher: the clasp. Available in three lengths, the filigree silver chains end in a colourfully encased bayonet clasp that is a statement in its own right. Thanks to the twisting mechanism, several chains can easily be linked together to create different lengths and a personal, individual mix of colours.

HERSTELLER / MANUFACTURER
bKing Design
Zwiesel

DESIGN
Inhouse
Bernadett King

VERTRIEB / DISTRIBUTOR
bKing Design
Zwiesel

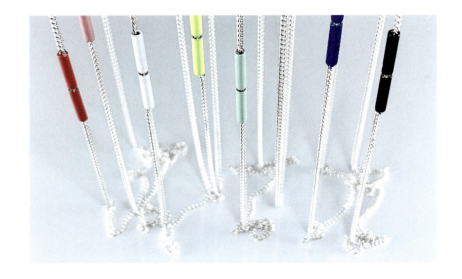

SPECIAL MENTION | BELVEDERE | BARKOLLEKTION / BAR COLLECTION

JURY STATEMENT

Hier wurde das Prinzip der Kannelur durchgängig über die ganze Kollektion angewendet, ein konsequenter Gestaltungsansatz. Zusammen mit dem Silber ergibt sich eine sehr hochwertige Anmutung.

A consistent design approach that applies the fluting principle to the entire collection. In combination with the silver, it results in an extremely upscale look.

HERSTELLER / MANUFACTURER
Robbe & Berking Silbermanufaktur seit 1874 GmbH & Co. KG
Flensburg

DESIGN
Inhouse

VERTRIEB / DISTRIBUTOR
Robbe & Berking Silbermanufaktur seit 1874 GmbH & Co. KG
Flensburg

Die Barkollektion wurde eigens entwickelt, um den stilvollen Genuss eines Drinks zu zelebrieren. Ob das gepflegte Feierabendbier, das festliche Glas Champagner oder ein Wodka on the Rocks – für jedes Getränk lässt sich aus den unterschiedlichsten Kelch- und Becherformen das passende Gefäß finden. Das Erscheinungsbild der versilberten Trinkgefäße erinnert an die Kanneluren antiker Säulen. Die charakteristische Oberflächenbeschaffenheit macht das Greifen und Halten angenehm, zudem übermittelt das Material durch seine hohe Temperaturleitfähigkeit sofort die Kühle des Getränks an Hand und Mund.

The bar collection was specially developed to promote the stylish enjoyment of a drink. The appearance of the silver-plated collection evokes the fluting of classical columns. This distinctive surface finish makes the vessels pleasant to pick up and hold, and thanks to its high thermal conductivity the material immediately conveys the coldness of the drink to hand and mouth.

SUSANNE EWERT **ZIELFORM LONDONBERLIN, BERLIN**

»Für mich war die Vielfalt der Einreichungen sehr spannend, erstens waren viele Produkte aus Deutschland zu sehen und zweitens interessante Produkte dabei, die bei anderen Wettbewerben nicht unbedingt vertreten sind. Das liegt sicherlich auch daran, dass der Focus Open einer der wenigen staatlichen deutschen Design-Wettbewerbe mit internationaler Ausrichtung ist.«

»For me, the diversity of the entries was really intriguing: for one thing there were a lot of products from Germany, and for another they included some interesting products that aren't necessarily represented in other competitions. I'm sure that's got something to do with the fact that Focus Open is Germany's only state-sponsored design competition with an international orientation.«

Susanne Ewert studierte Industrial Design an der heutigen Muthesius Kunsthochschule Kiel. Mit ihrem Geschäftspartner und Designer, Clemens Koschel, entwickelt sie heute innovative Produkte für den Konsum-, Medizin- und Investitionsgüterbereich – von der Produktkonzeption bis einschließlich der konstruktiven Umsetzung. Viele ihrer Designs, etwa für elgato, Sennheiser, Söhnle und Lunos wurden mit Designpreisen ausgezeichnet. Susanne Ewert engagiert sich ehrenamtlich als Mitglied der Adhoc AG für Nachhaltigkeit (Agenda 2030) des Deutschen Kulturrates und vertritt den VDID als Rätin im Rat für Nachhaltigkeit des Deutschen Designertag.

www.zielform-london.berlin

Susanne Ewert studied industrial design in Kiel at what is today the Muthesius University of Fine Arts and Design. Together with her business partner, designer Clemens Koschel, she develops innovative products for the consumer, medical and capital goods sectors – from the conception of the product all the way to the engineering design. Many of her designs for clients such as elgato, Sennheiser, Söhnle and Lunos have been honoured with design accolades. Susanne Ewert works in a voluntary capacity as a member of the German Cultural Council's Adhoc AG for Sustainability (Agenda 2030) and represents the VDID (Association of German Industrial Designers) on the Deutscher Designtag's Council for Sustainability.

www.zielform-london.berlin

1 → SEITE / PAGE
114–119

2 → SEITE / PAGE
120, 124

3 → SEITE / PAGE
121, 125

4 → SEITE / PAGE
122, 126

LICHT
LIGHTING

1	**GOLD:** **Q FOUR** Nimbus Group GmbH Stuttgart
2	**SPECIAL MENTION:** **TOLOU** Steng Licht GmbH Kernen
3	**REFLEX² CEILING** Serien Raumleuchten GmbH Rodgau
4	**BOLOGNA** Mawa Design Licht- und Wohnideen Michendorf

Licht aus der Leuchtdiode ist längst Standard – denn sie bietet nicht nur Energieeffizienz, sie ermöglicht auch ganzheitlich konzipierte Leuchtensysteme. Neben der Ergänzung mit zusätzlichen Features oder der faszinierenden Miniaturisierung bietet das Halbleiter-Leuchtmittel die Möglichkeit, auch einzelne Leuchten in digitale Steuerungssysteme zu integrieren.

Light-emitting diodes have long since become a standard light source – in addition to being energy-efficient, they permit holistically designed lighting systems as well. Besides enabling additional features and a fascinating degree of miniaturisation, the semiconductor light source also provides the option of integrating individual luminaires into digital control systems.

GOLD Q FOUR LEUCHTENFAMILIE
LUMINAIRE FAMILY

Q FOUR

LEUCHTEN
FAMILIE

LICHT
LIGHTING

FOCUS
GOLD

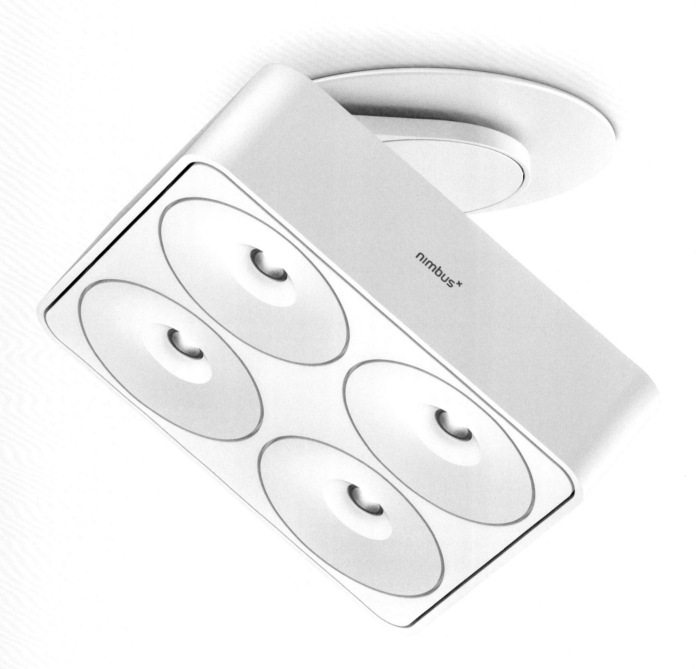

GOLD Q FOUR LEUCHTENFAMILIE / LUMINAIRE FAMILY

JURY STATEMENT

Ein herausragendes Beispiel für Invisible Light, für Licht also, das seine Quelle zunächst nicht offenbart, weil diese keine Streuung produziert. Mit seinen vier formal absolut reduzierten Varianten bleibt das System überschaubar, bietet aber ausreichend Optionen für unterschiedliche Szenarien.

An outstanding example of invisible light, meaning light that does not immediately reveal where it comes from because its source does not produce scattering. With just four extremely minimalist variants, the system is pleasantly straightforward but nevertheless provides sufficient options for creating different scenarios.

HERSTELLER / MANUFACTURER
Nimbus Group GmbH
Stuttgart

DESIGN
Inhouse

VERTRIEB / DISTRIBUTOR
Nimbus Group GmbH
Stuttgart

Speziell entwickelte Linsen ermöglichen es, das LED-Licht fast ohne Streulicht zu fokussieren. Zugleich sorgen der kleine Lichtaustritt und die Entblendung dafür, dass die vier LED-Lichtquellen nicht wirklich erkennbar sind. Der Lichtstrom scheint also direkt aus einer Blackbox zu kommen und wirkt als präzise gesetzter Hellwert auf den zu illuminierenden Flächen, die damit besonders brillant anmuten. Die Entblendung verleiht der Innenbeleuchtung gläserner Architektur eine neue Qualität, da sie Reflektionen auf den Scheiben ausschließt.

Die Leuchtenfamilie umfasst insgesamt vier Modelle: ein Aufbau-Downlight, die Einbauversion, die dreh- und schwenkbare Aufbauvariante sowie die Stromschienen-Version. Damit lassen sich verschiedenste Lichtszenarien mit einem Leuchten-Grundtypus realisieren. Abmessungen und Radien nehmen überdies Bezug auf das Modul Q 36, einen über zehn Jahre alten Klassiker des Unternehmens.

Specially developed lenses make it possible to focus the LED light almost entirely without scattering. In addition, the small openings through which the light is emitted and glare suppression ensure that the four LED light sources are not really discernible as such. As a result, the light appears to come straight out of a black box and creates precisely defined areas of brightness on the surfaces to be illuminated, making them look unusually brilliant. The glare suppression brings a new quality to interior lighting for glass architecture because it eliminates reflections on the panes.

The luminaire family consists of four models: a surface-mounted downlight, a recessed version, a rotatable and tiltable variant of the surface-mounted model and a version for track systems. As a result, a wide range of different lighting scenarios can be created with one basic type of luminaire. In addition, the dimensions and radius corners echo those of Modul Q 36, a classic that the company launched more than 10 years ago.

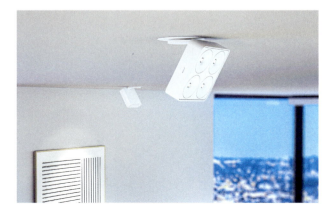

DIETRICH F. BRENNENSTUHL **GESCHÄFTSFÜHRER, NIMBUS GROUP GMBH**

»Die Gestaltung leitet sich von den verschiedenen technischen, aber auch anwendungsspezifischen Faktoren ab.«

»The design is derived from various technical aspects, as well as application-specific factors.«

DIETRICH F. BRENNENSTUHL **MANAGING DIRECTOR, NIMBUS GROUP GMBH**

→ **Wie produziert man Licht, das lediglich auf der zu beleuchtenden Fläche präsent ist?**
Wir beschäftigen uns schon lange mit der Entblendung sowie der Ausgewogenheit aus Streuung und Fokussierung. Neu ist, die Lichtquelle gänzlich verschwinden zu lassen, gleichzeitig ein fokussiertes Licht zu bekommen und nicht nur eine indirekt strahlende Wirkung. Der Einstieg zu diesem Thema war unser Lighting Pad. Wir haben die Lichtquellen in der Täler- und Hügellandschaft versenkt und damit dem Auge des Betrachters entzogen. Dieses Prinzip haben wir dann auf die Q Four übertragen und mit vier Linsen gekoppelt.

Die Lichtquelle bleibt nahezu unsichtbar – sollte das Design der Leuchte ebenso reduziert sein?
Das kommt ein Stück weit auf den Einsatzbereich an. Eine Esstischleuchte sollte meiner Ansicht nach sehr entblendet sein, ich möchte bei der Betrachtung meines Gegenübers keine Kringel auf der Netzhaut sehen. Aber die Gestalt der Leuchte darf eine bewusste Präsenz besitzen, die etwas mit dem Raum über und auf dem Tisch bewirkt. Daher haben wir unserem Lighting Pad Lounge eine ungewöhnliche Größe gegeben und bezeichnen die Leuchte daher auch als Lichtmöbel. Die Einbauversion der Q Four verschwindet dagegen förmlich in der Decke.

Wie eng arbeiten bei Nimbus die technische Entwicklung und das Design zusammen?
Form follows Function – das stimmt in vielen Bereichen unseres Schaffens. Das heißt, die Gestaltung leitet sich von den verschiedenen technischen, aber auch anwendungsspezifischen Faktoren ab. Natürlich hat der Gestalter von Anfang an ein grobes Bild der Gestaltung vor Augen. Aber die eigentliche Ausprägung entsteht stark getrieben durch die Funktion. Einziger Ausreißer in unserem Programm war die Leuchte Squeeze von Karim Rashid, mit der wir aber bewusst polarisieren und provozieren wollten.

Wie wichtig ist der Systemgedanke bei der Entwicklung von Leuchten, also das Angebot von Varianten?
Die LED hat uns vor 15 Jahren wie ein Werkzeug den neuen Umgang mit Licht ermöglicht. Lichtlinien im Raum, aber auch an oder in Möbeln beeinflussen die Gesamtlichtkonzepte. Daraus entstehen neue Archetypen von Lichtquellen, die dann als Derivate einer Grundidee die komplette Beleuchtung von Räumen erfassen können.
So gesehen ist die Linse der Q Four und des Lighting Pads auch eine Art Archetyp, den wir in Derivaten weiterdenken. Das sind evolutionäre Schritte für Innovationen und damit für andere, neue, spannende Lichterlebnisse. Schließlich ist die Wahrnehmung von Licht im Raum nicht statisch, sondern verändert sich – wie alle Dinge und Themen, die uns täglich umgeben.

Der Architekt Dietrich F. Brennenstuhl hat Nimbus 1988 gegründet. Als einer der ersten Unternehmen der Lichtbranche hat Nimbus bereits 2006 die LED aufgegriffen und sein Portfolio darauf umgestellt. Nimbus gehört zu den regelmäßigen Preisträgern des Focus Open und ist seit 2019 Teil des Nagolder Familienunternehmens Häfele.

www.nimbus-lighting.com

→ **How do you produce light that is only present on the surface to be illuminated?**
We've been concentrating on glare suppression and achieving a balance between scattering and focus for a long time now. Making the light source disappear completely while simultaneously producing focused light rather than just an indirect effect is new. Our Lighting Pad was the first step in that direction. We countersank the light sources in the hill-and-valley landscape, which made them invisible to the beholder. Then we transferred the same principle to the Q Four and paired it with four lenses.

The light source is virtually invisible – is the design of the luminaire intended to be equally understated?
It depends on the area of application to some extent. In my opinion, a luminaire over a dining table should produce very little glare, I don't want to see rings on the retina of the person sitting opposite me. But it's fine for the design of the luminaire to have a deliberate presence that has a certain impact on the space above and on the table. That's why we made our Lighting Pad Lounge an unusual size and describe the luminaire as »light furniture«. By contrast, the recessed version of the Q Four literally disappears into the ceiling.

How close is the collaboration between technical development and design at Nimbus?
Form follows function – that applies to many areas of our creative work. That means the design is derived from various technical aspects, as well as application-specific factors. Obviously the designer has a rough idea of the design in mind right from the start. But the final form is very much driven by the function. The only outlier in our collection was the Squeeze luminaire by Karim Rashid, but that was a very deliberate attempt to polarise and provoke.

When you're developing luminaires, how important is it for you to come up with a system-based concept, i.e. a collection that offers different variations on a theme?
When the LED came on the scene 15 years ago, it was like a tool that enabled us to treat light in a new way. Lines of light in space, but also on or in furniture, have an impact on the overall lighting concept. That gives rise to new archetypes of light sources; then, as derivatives of a basic idea, they can be used to meet the complete illumination needs of entire spaces.
Seen from that perspective, the lens of the Q Four and Lighting Pad is also a kind of archetype that we're developing in the form of derivatives. They're evolutionary steps for innovations and therefore also for new, different and intriguing light experiences. Ultimately, the way we perceive light in a space isn't static, it changes – like all the things and themes we're surrounded with in everyday life.

Architect Dietrich F. Brennenstuhl founded Nimbus in 1988. As early as 2006, Nimbus became one of the first companies in the lighting sector to embrace LEDs and adapt its portfolio accordingly. Nimbus regularly numbers among the winners of the Focus Open awards and has been part of Nagold-based family-run company Häfele since 2019.

www.nimbus-lighting.com

SPECIAL MENTION | TOLOU | PENDELLEUCHTE / PENDANT LUMINAIRE

→ SEITE / PAGE 124

SPECIAL MENTION | REFLEX² CEILING → SEITE / PAGE 125 | DECKENLEUCHTE CEILING LUMINAIRE

SPECIAL MENTION | BOLOGNA → SEITE / PAGE 126 | STEHLEUCHTE FLOOR LAMP

SPECIAL MENTION TOLOU PENDELLEUCHTE / PENDANT LUMINAIRE

JURY STATEMENT

Mit ihrem textilbezogenen Schirm orientiert sich die Pendelleuchte auf den ersten Blick an klassischen Modellen. Andererseits löst sie sich von diesen durch die filigrane Ringform und den schwebenden Charakter. Besonders interessant ist die Abhängung mit der rollengeführten Umlenkung des Netzkabels.

At first glance, the pendant luminaire's textile-covered shade is reminiscent of classic models. On the other hand, its slender ring shape and floating character set it apart. The pulley used to guide the cable adds a particularly interesting touch to the suspension system.

Die Formensprache der ringförmigen Pendelleuchte ist sachlich und klar – einen ganz eigenen, unverwechselbaren Look erhält sie durch die textile Bespannung von Schirm und Baldachin. Lediglich ein filigranes Stahlseil hält die Leuchte, zusammen mit einer kleinen Umlenkrolle, in Balance, was ihr einen fast schwebenden Charakter verleiht. Die Ausführung der Rolle in Chrom, goldfarben oder rot lackiert, steht dabei in bewusstem Materialkontrast zur seidenmatten Textilbespannung.

Integrierte LEDs geben Licht sowohl nach unten wie auch nach oben ab. Ihre Lichtstärke lässt sich – auch nach Up- und Downlight getrennt – entweder über einen Dimmer oder per App regeln.

The design language of the ring-shaped pendant luminaire is clear and objective – and is given a very unique, distinctive look by the textile covering of the shade and canopy. Nothing but a slender steel cable and a little pulley keep the luminaire in balance, giving it an almost floating character. The pulley is available with a chrome, gold or red lacquer finish – a deliberate contrast with the material of the semi-matt textile covering.

The integrated LEDs emit both upward and downward light. Their intensity is regulated either by a dimmer or an app, with the possibility of controlling the uplight and downlight separately.

HERSTELLER / MANUFACTURER
Steng Licht GmbH
Kernen

DESIGN
Designstudio Speziell
Offenbach

VERTRIEB / DISTRIBUTOR
Steng Licht GmbH
Kernen

SPECIAL MENTION

REFLEX² CEILING
DECKENLEUCHTE
CEILING LUMINAIRE

JURY STATEMENT

Die Leuchte ist physisch extrem reduziert und nur durch ihren schattenwerfenden Wireframe präsent. Erst im Betrieb wird sie körperhafter, wobei die Quelle des weichen Lichts versteckt bleibt. Eigentlich besteht die Leuchte nur aus Licht.

In physical terms, the luminaire is reduced to a minimum, present only in the form of its shadow-casting wireframe. It only becomes more tangible when in use, although the source of the soft light remains hidden from view. Essentially, the luminaire consists of nothing but light.

HERSTELLER/MANUFACTURER
Serien Raumleuchten GmbH
Rodgau

DESIGN
Inhouse

VERTRIEB/DISTRIBUTOR
Serien Raumleuchten GmbH
Rodgau

Die Deckenleuchte ist Bestandteil einer Produktfamilie, zu der auch Deckenfluter und Wandleuchten gehören. Allen gemeinsam ist die reduzierte Ästhetik einer minimalistischen Rahmenstruktur aus Aluminium, in die LED-Platinen eingebettet sind. Sie strahlen auf eine anschlussseitig integrierte, prismatische Reflektorfläche im gleichen Grundmaß, die auch bei voller Leistung für absolut blendfreies Licht sorgt. Die Lichttemperatur lässt sich per Klick über eine App steuern, eine einfache Montage und die Möglichkeit, LEDs und Reflektor einfach auszutauschen, setzen Statements in puncto Nachhaltigkeit.

The ceiling luminaire is part of a product family that also includes uplighters and wall lamps. What they all have in common is the understated aesthetic of a minimalist aluminium frame structure with LED boards embedded in it. Their light shines onto a prismatic reflector with the same basic measurements that is integrated on the ceiling side of the board, ensuring totally glare-free light even at full brightness. The colour temperature is controlled via an app, installation is straightforward and the simple replacement of both the LEDs and reflector is a statement about sustainability.

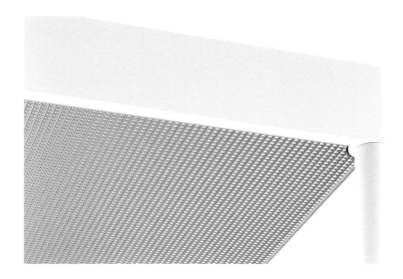

SPECIAL MENTION BOLOGNA STEHLEUCHTE FLOOR LAMP

JURY STATEMENT

Stilistisch spielt diese Leuchte in einer ganz eigenständigen Liga. Faszinierend wirkt der große Glaskörper und die hohe Fertigungspräzision, alle Details sind perfekt ausgeführt: Die physische Erscheinung und die Lichtwirkung machen die Leuchte zu einem besonderen Raumelement.

Stylistically, this luminaire is in a league of its own. The large glass vessel and the precision that has gone into its production are fascinating, every detail is perfect: its physical appearance and the lighting effect make this luminaire a very special element of the interior.

HERSTELLER/MANUFACTURER
Mawa Design
Licht- und Wohnideen
Michendorf

DESIGN
Inhouse
und/and
Aloys F. Gangkofner †
Michendorf

VERTRIEB/DISTRIBUTOR
Mawa Design
Licht- und Wohnideen
Michendorf

Die filigrane Rippenstruktur des voluminösen Überfangglases erinnert an einen Lampion – nur, dass dieser nicht in luftigen Höhen hängt, sondern bodennah fest auf einem metallenen Dreifuß verankert ist. Der handgefertigte Glaskörper orientiert sich an Entwürfen des Glasgestalters Aloys F. Gangkofner aus den 1950er- und 1960er-Jahren. Seine milchige Einfärbung erzeugt zusammen mit dem integrierten LED-dim2warm-Leuchtmittel ein sehr atmosphärisches Licht. Die LED-Technik erreicht einen Lichtstrom von bis zu 806 Lumen und lässt sich mittels eines Fußdimmers stufenlos und flackerfrei dimmen. Eine abnehmbare Abdeckung schützt das Innere der Leuchte und ermöglicht den einfachen Austausch des Leuchtmittels.

The delicate ribbed texture of the voluminous flashed glass shade is evocative of a Chinese lantern – except that rather than hanging in the air it hovers close to the floor, permanently anchored to a metal tripod. The handmade glass vessel is based on designs by Aloys F. Gangkofner from the 1950s and 1960s. Together with the integrated LED dim2warm light source, its milky colouring creates an extremely atmospheric light. The LED technology produces luminous flux of up to 806 lumens; a foot switch is used to control the seamless, flicker-free dimming function. A removable cover protects the inside of the luminaire and provides easy access when the light source needs changing.

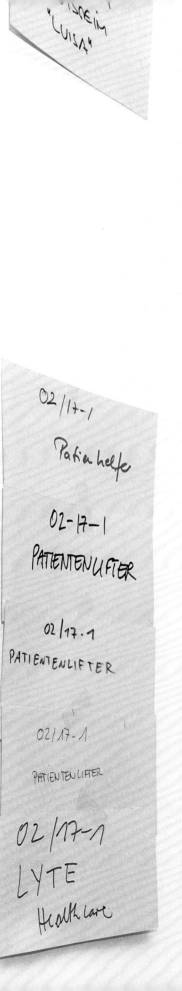

  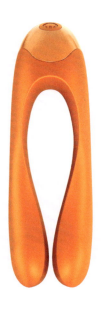

1 → **SEITE / PAGE** 130–135

2 → **SEITE / PAGE** 136–141

3 → **SEITE / PAGE** 142, 146

4 → **SEITE / PAGE** 143, 147

5 → **SEITE / PAGE** 144, 148

FREIZEIT, SPORT, SPIELEN
LEISURE, SPORTS, PLAY

1 **GOLD:**
   NL PURE
   Swarovski Optik KG
   Absam
   Österreich / Austria

2 **M99 DY PRO**
   Supernova Design
   GmbH & Co. KG
   Gundelfingen

3 **SILVER:**
   CANDY CANE
   Eis GmbH
   Bielefeld

4 **SPECIAL MENTION:**
   ULTRA POWER BULLET 5
   Eis GmbH
   Bielefeld

5 **KICKERLAND**
   STECKKICKER
   b+a Vertriebs GmbH
   Ilsfeld

Einst Leerraum für Entspannung, Rekreation und absichtsloses Sein, ist die Freizeit längst prall gefüllt mit Aktivitätsangeboten und entsprechenden Produkten für unterschiedlichste Neigungen, Altersgruppen und Erlebnisversprechen. Schön, wenn es da Dinge gibt, die keinen unmittelbaren Zweck erfüllen wollen – oder das Naturerlebnis intensivieren.

Whereas free time was once a vacuum waiting to be filled with relaxation, recreation and delectable idleness, today it is crammed full with a vast spectrum of activity options and the corresponding products for diverse inclinations, age groups and experiences. Every now and again, it's nice when there are things that serve no direct purpose – or intensify the way we experience nature.

GOLD   NL PURE   FERNGLÄSER
BINOCULARS

NL PURE
FERNGLÄSER

FOCUS GOLD

FREIZEIT, SPORT, SPIELEN
LEISURE, SPORTS, PLAY

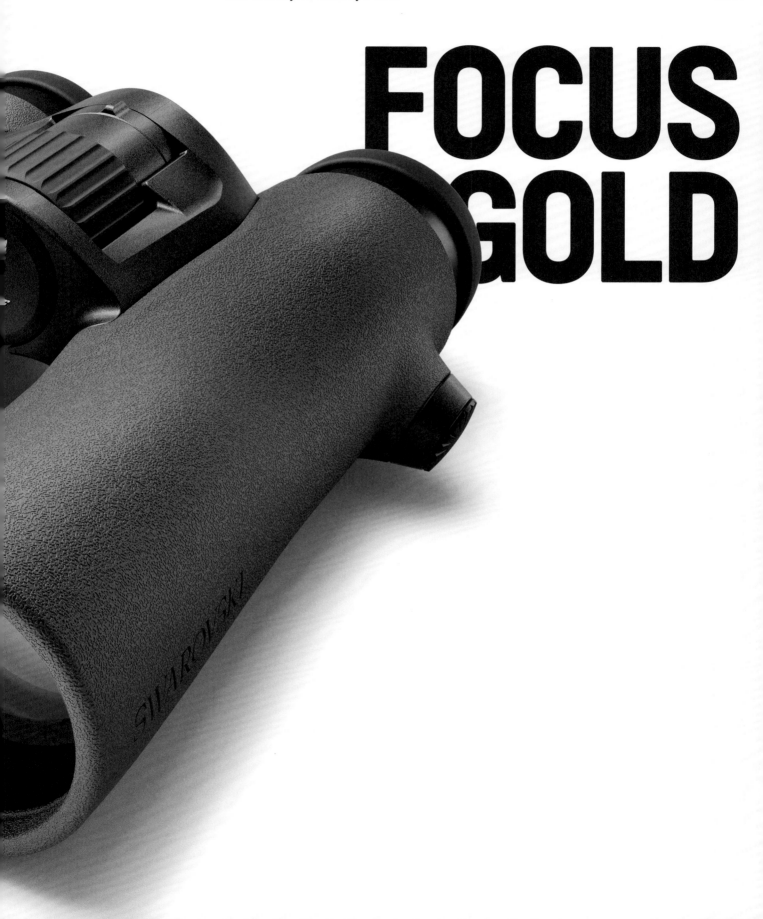

GOLD — NL PURE — FERNGLÄSER / BINOCULARS

JURY STATEMENT

Die Fernglas-Familie ist bestens aufeinander abgestimmt und verknüpft die formal sehr saubere Gestaltung mit neuen ergonomischen Ansätzen, die das Handling spürbar verbessern. Den praktischen Gedanken nehmen die unverlierbaren Schutzkappen auf, mit denen sich die wertvolle Optik trefflich schützen lässt.

The range of binoculars is extremely well coordinated and combines an immaculate design with new ergonomic approaches that noticeably improve handling. The practical focus is echoed in the unlosable caps that provide excellent protection for the valuable lenses.

HERSTELLER/MANUFACTURER
Swarovski Optik KG
Absam
Österreich/Austria

DESIGN
Formquadrat GmbH
Linz
Österreich/Austria

VERTRIEB/DISTRIBUTOR
Swarovski Optik KG
Absam
Österreich/Austria

Primär für die Naturbeobachtung konzipiert sind die acht-, zehn- und zwölffach vergrößernden Ferngläser – folgerichtig dominierten maximale optische und ergonomische Qualitäten die Entwicklung. Die Gehäuse sind beispielsweise nicht zylindrisch aufgebaut, sondern so geformt, dass sie die natürliche Greifhaltung der Nutzer*innen unterstützen. Dies und die optionale, neu entwickelte Stirnstütze machen Langzeitbeobachtungen komfortabler, ebenso wie der kaum wahrnehmbare Sehfeldrand und das augenseitige, 71 Grad weite Sehfeld. Die kompakte Mechanik inklusive gesondertem Dioptrienausgleich ist auf Langlebigkeit ausgelegt. Mit 840 Gramm Gewicht und 158 Millimeter Länge bleiben die Ferngläser sehr gut handhabbar.

With 8x, 10x and 12x magnification, the binoculars are primarily intended for nature-watching – which is why their development focused on maximum optical and ergonomic qualities. Rather than being cylindrical, for instance, the housings are shaped to fit the user's hands so that they can be held naturally. Together with the optional, newly developed forehead rest, they make prolonged observation more comfortable, as do the barely perceptible edges of the field of view and the 71 degree apparent field of view. The compact mechanism, including the separate dioptre adjustment, is designed to last. Weighing 840 grams and measuring 158 millimetres in length, the binoculars are also very easy to handle.

MARIO ZEPPETZAUER **GESELLSCHAFTER, FORMQUADRAT GMBH**

»Es war notwendig, Teile des Fernglases von Grund auf neu zu denken.«

»It was necessary to rethink parts of the binoculars from scratch.«

links / left: Julian Pröll
rechts / right: Mario Zeppetzauer
Foto / Photo: Michael Liebert

MARIO ZEPPETZAUER
PARTNER, FORMQUADRAT GMBH

→ **Die Form eines Fernglases ist eigentlich funktional vorbestimmt. Wo kann das Design ansetzen?**
Betrachtet man ein Fernglas mit seinen kreisförmigen Linsen, so liegt der Schluss nahe, jedes Fernglas bestehe aus zwei Zylindern. Gutes Design hat den Anspruch, alles zu hinterfragen, auch das vermeintlich Gegebene. Zwischen dem Okular und dem Objektiv werden Prismen verbaut, welche die Zylinderform nicht voll ausfüllen. Genau an diesen Stellen haben wir angesetzt, um die Ergonomie zu verbessern. Um den Entwurf umzusetzen, war es auch in der technischen Entwicklung notwendig, Teile des Fernglases von Grund auf neu zu denken – letztendlich war es eine Teamleistung.

Wie definiert man die Usability bei einem optischen Präzisionsprodukt wie einem Fernglas?
Die Usability entsteht aus der Summe der einzelnen Teile. Es gibt nicht die eine Maßnahme, um die Schnittstelle zwischen Mensch und Produkt bestmöglich zu gestalten. Bei der optischen Usability etwa geht es um Sehfeld, Lichtstärke, Dämmerungszahl, Farbwiedergabe, Transmission. Für eine Handhabung über einen langen Zeitraum wird um jedes Gramm gekämpft und kompromissloser Leichtbau betrieben. Bedienelemente wie das Fokussierrad müssen an der ergonomisch richtigen Position liegen und eine kontrollierte Leichtgängigkeit aufweisen, damit User*in und Produkt »zusammenwachsen«.

Welche Herausforderungen gab es beim Gestaltungsprozess zu meistern?
Ziel war, die optische Leistung und Ergonomie des Fernglases auf eine neue Stufe zu stellen und pionierhaft die Grenzen des Machbaren zu verschieben. Für die Gestaltung stand nur ein Spielraum von wenigen Millimetern zur Verfügung. Es galt, Wege abseits bekannter, logischer Herangehensweisen zu finden, explorativ in Richtungen zu denken, in denen noch keine Lösung in Sicht war und zu erkennen, dass das Ziel nur interdisziplinär und gemeinsam durch Entwicklungsabteilung und Gestalter erreicht werden kann.

Und wie nachhaltig kann ein Fernglas sein?
Gute Ferngläser gehören zur Sparte der Premiumprodukte. Sie werden intensiv genutzt und über Generationen weitergegeben. Die Länge und Intensität der Produktnutzung gehören zu den wichtigsten Hebeln für mehr Nachhaltigkeit. Als produzierendes Unternehmen, das auf Ressourcen aus der Natur angewiesen ist, produziert Swarovski Optik am Produktionsstandort in Tirol auf eine möglichst umweltfreundliche und ressourcenschonende Weise.

Gegründet von Stefan Degn und Mario Zeppetzauer, steht Formquadrat seit 20 Jahren für die Gestaltung technischer Produkte, die vielfach ausgezeichnet und in den Märkten erfolgreich sind.

Swarovski Optik mit Sitz in Absam, Tirol, ist Teil der Unternehmensgruppe Swarovski. Das 1949 gegründete, österreichische Unternehmen ist auf die Entwicklung und Herstellung fernoptischer Geräte von höchster Präzision spezialisiert.

www.formquadrat.com
www.swarovskioptik.com

→ **The form of a pair of binoculars is actually predetermined by their function. Where can design come into the equation?**
If you look at binoculars and their circular lenses, the obvious conclusion is that every pair of binoculars must consist of two cylinders. But good design should question everything, even things that seem like givens. Between the eyepiece and the objective there are prisms that don't quite fill the cylindrical shape. And that was our starting point for improving the ergonomics. In order for the design to be implemented, the technical development engineers had to rethink parts of the binoculars from scratch – at the end of the day, it was a team effort.

How do you define usability when it comes to a high-precision optical product like binoculars?
Usability results from the sum of the individual parts. There's no one single step you can take that ensures the interface between user and product is designed in the best possible way. Optical usability involves things like field of view, relative brightness, twilight factor, colour fidelity and light transmission. When the binoculars are to be used for extended periods, every gram counts and the design needs to ensure they're as lightweight as possible. Elements like the focusing wheel have to be positioned where they make the most ergonomic sense and be easy – but not too easy – to adjust so that the user and product »grow together«.

What challenges did you have to overcome during the design process?
The goal was to take the optical performance and ergonomics of binoculars to a new level, push the envelope and come up with a pioneering result. As far as the design was concerned, we only had a few millimetres to play with. It was a question of finding ways to do that beyond the familiar, logical approaches, of being explorative and thinking in new directions with no solution in sight when we started out, and of realising that the only way to achieve the goal was for the development department and designers to come together as an interdisciplinary team.

And how sustainable can binoculars be?
Good binoculars belong in the premium products category. They're used intensively and handed down from one generation to the next. The duration and intensity of product usage are among the most important levers for ensuring greater sustainability. As a manufacturing company that depends on resources from nature, Swarovski Optik ensures that the processes used at its production site in Tyrol are as eco-friendly and resource-efficient as possible.

Founded by Stefan Degn and Mario Zeppetzauer, Formquadrat has been designing technical products that win awards and succeed on the market for 20 years.

Swarovski Optik is based in Absam, Tyrol, and is part of the Swarovski Group. Founded in 1949, the Austrian company specialises in the development and manufacture of long-range optical products of the highest precision.

www.formquadrat.com
www.swarovskioptik.com

GOLD   M99 DY PRO   **FAHRRADSCHEINWERFER
BICYCLE HEADLIGHT**

M99
DY PRO

M99 DY PRO

FREIZEIT, SPORT, SPIELEN
LEISURE, SPORTS, PLAY

FOCUS GOLD

FAHRRAD-SCHEINWERFER

GOLD — M99 DY PRO — FAHRRADSCHEINWERFER / BICYCLE HEADLIGHT

JURY STATEMENT

Formal baut dieser Scheinwerfer auf anderen Modellen des Herstellers auf. Seine Rippung im hinteren Bereich, die breite Front und der facettierte Reflektor – eigentlich technische Aspekte – werden zu klaren, modellübergreifenden Designmerkmalen. Das eloxierte Finish ist genauso perfekt wie die Montage mit schlanken Schellen. Und: Der Hersteller verspricht eine zehnjährige Reparierbarkeit.

The form of this headlight echoes that of other models from the same manufacturer. The ribbing at the back, wide front and facetted reflector – which are actually technical aspects – double as distinctive design features that are common to all models. The anodised finish is just as perfect as the slender clips used to mount it. What's more, the headlight comes with a 10-year repairability promise.

HERSTELLER/MANUFACTURER
Supernova Design GmbH & Co. KG
Gundelfingen

DESIGN
Inhouse

VERTRIEB/DISTRIBUTOR
Supernova Design GmbH & Co. KG
Gundelfingen

Das Fahrrad ist auf dem besten Weg, zu einem echten Transportmittel für den Alltag zu werden. Entscheidend dabei ist, wie es gelingt, das Radfahren sicherer zu machen. Die Beleuchtung spielt dabei eine große Rolle, hat sie doch einen doppelten Effekt: Ein leistungsfähiger Scheinwerfer sorgt für mehr Sicht im Dunkeln und für eine bessere Wahrnehmung im Verkehr. Mit seiner Kombination aus Tagfahr-, Abblend- und Fernlicht erfüllt dieser Scheinwerfer die wichtigsten Voraussetzungen für mehr Sicherheit. Die leistungsfähigen LEDs sorgen für enorme Helligkeiten und beziehen ihre Energie erstmals aus handelsüblichen Nabendynamos. Fernlicht, bislang E-Bikern vorbehalten, ist nun auch für motorlose Fahrräder erhältlich – und sogar mit StVZO-Zulassung. Ein Sensor schaltet automatisch zwischen Tagfahr- und Abblendlicht um, das Fernlicht wird über einen beleuchteten, frei montierbaren Taster aktiviert.

The bicycle is well on its way to becoming a genuine means of transport for everyday life. Finding ways to make cycling safer will play a crucial role in that. The lights are of key importance because they have a two-fold effect: a high-performance headlight not only ensures the rider can see better in the dark, it also means they are more visible to other road users. With its combination of daytime running, low-beam and high-beam modes, this headlight meets the most important requirements for greater safety. The high-performance LEDs produce huge levels of brightness and, for the first time, are powered by conventional hub dynamos. High-beam mode, hitherto reserved for e-bikes, is now available for motorless bikes too – and is even approved as road-legal under German road traffic licensing regulations. A sensor automatically switches between daytime running and low beam mode, while the high beam is activated by means of an illuminated switch that can be positioned as required.

MARCUS WALLMEYER CEO UND HEAD OF DESIGN,
SUPERNOVA DESIGN GMBH & CO. KG

»Eine gelungene Formensprache muss nicht ständig geändert werden.«

»There's no need to keep changing a successful design language.«

MARCUS WALLMEYER

MARCUS WALLMEYER
CEO AND HEAD OF DESIGN, SUPERNOVA DESIGN GMBH & CO. KG

→ **Mr Wallmeyer, this is your fourth Gold award in a row – what's your secret?**

As owner of the company and an active cyclist, I'm in the fortunate position of being able to implement my designs just the way I want them. There are probably very few designers who can do that.

In terms of form, there are strong links between this year's award-winning headlight and last year's winning model. How important is the continuity of your design language to you?

There are technical reasons for the form too, of course, which continue to apply and determine the design. But quite apart from that, there's no need to keep changing a successful design language. The better the design is, the more universal it is and the longer it can be used. Customers like the fact that it's a strong recognition factor.

You seem to have an inexhaustible supply of product ideas – what triggers the start of a development?

It varies a lot. It might start with a personal night-time ride or new technologies that we'd like to deploy. With the M99 DY PRO, we brought our dynamo headlight bang up to date. It's been very successful for more than 10 years now, but instead of just implementing an evolutionary improvement we totally revisited the whole thing. Our electronic engineers developed a completely new, highly efficient electronics architecture that gets enough energy out of the normal dynamo to power a high beam. That's an absolute first.

You're designer and entrepreneur in one – which role do you mainly see yourself in?

Design and development are my biggest passion, but it's also great fun to influence entire market segments with new developments.

Bikes are considered a sustainable means of transport, but if you look at the industry itself you can't help wondering sometimes … Do you think the bike industry itself needs to become more sustainable?

There's definitely still lots of room for improvement, and the industry has realised that and is working on it. For quite a while now, we've been investing a lot of time and money in making the products, production processes and supply chain more eco-friendly. One important aspect that's often neglected is a product's lifespan. All our products are designed to have a useful life of 10 years and can still be repaired even after the five-year guarantee expires. Our customers regularly send in even older headlights and ask us to give them an overhaul.

Otherwise, we're a member of the Biodiversity Partnership Mesoamerica and support the reforestation of the rain forest with all sorts of different tree species. We want to combine carbon offsetting with an ecologically valuable impact.

Because he wanted to be able to train for extended periods at night too, founder and racing cyclist Marcus Wallmeyer built his first bicycle headlight back in 1995 – out of a tomato puree can and a motorbike battery. Nowadays the company employs over 50 people and produces high-performance light systems for bikes with and without an electric motor on an industrial scale. In addition, Supernova continues to take on design assignments from third-party customers.

www.supernova-lights.com

SILVER   CANDY CANE   SEXTOY
                            SEX TOY
          → SEITE / PAGE
            146

SPECIAL MENTION | ULTRA POWER BULLET 5 → SEITE / PAGE 147 | SEXTOY SEX TOY

| SPECIAL MENTION | KICKERLAND STECKKICKER → SEITE / PAGE 148 | TISCHKICKER TABLE FOOTBALL |

SILVER

CANDY CANE

SEXTOY
SEX TOY

JURY STATEMENT

Ein sehr ästhetisches Produkt mit perfekten Flächenübergängen und einer assoziativen Formensprache. Dadurch wirkt das Toy nicht aufdringlich, sondern sehr diskret.

A very aesthetic product with perfect transitions between the surfaces and an associative design language. As a result, there is nothing blatant about the toy's appearance, which instead looks very discreet.

Der Fingervibrator aus medizinischem Silikon verspricht eine Vielzahl von Anwendungen für die sinnliche Zeit allein oder zu zweit. In den beiden biegsamen Armen, die bei Gebrauch den Mittelfinger umschließen, arbeitet jeweils ein leistungsstarker, dabei leiser Motor, der die Vibrationen auf diverse erogene Zonen überträgt. Per Bedienknopf lassen sich dabei zwölf Intensitätsstufen wählen. Ein integrierter Akku sorgt für umweltfreundliches Wiederaufladen, während die nahtlose Verarbeitung des Toys auch den problemlosen Einsatz im Wasser erlaubt.

Made of medical-grade silicone, the finger vibrator promises a multitude of uses for sensual enjoyment alone or with a partner. The two flexible arms, which surround the middle finger when in use, each contain a powerful but quiet motor that transmits the vibrations to various erogenous zones. A control button is used to select one of 12 different intensity levels. An integrated battery permits eco-friendly recharging, and thanks to its seamless surface the toy can be used in water as well.

HERSTELLER/MANUFACTURER
Eis GmbH
Bielefeld

DESIGN
Inhouse

VERTRIEB/DISTRIBUTOR
Eis GmbH
Bielefeld

SPECIAL MENTION

ULTRA POWER BULLET 5

SEXTOY / SEX TOY

JURY STATEMENT

Dieses Sextoy könnte auch eine Formstudie sein, quasi eine Art Kleinstskulptur. Es bleibt unauffällig, dezent und mutet edel an. Damit unterscheidet es sich wohltuend von plumperen Vertretern seiner Art.

This sex toy could almost be mistaken for a study in form, a kind of miniature sculpture, so to speak. It is unobtrusive, discreet and has an upscale appeal – a pleasant change from cruder examples of its kind.

HERSTELLER / MANUFACTURER
Eis GmbH
Bielefeld

DESIGN
Inhouse

VERTRIEB / DISTRIBUTOR
Eis GmbH
Bielefeld

Der Vibrator ist speziell für Frauen entwickelt und orientiert sich mit seiner zylindrischen, eleganten Formgebung an den Ansprüchen von Nutzerinnen, die Wert auf ästhetische und langlebige Lifestyleprodukte legen. Die handliche Größe sorgt zusammen mit der strukturierten Silikonoberfläche und der abgerundeten Spitze für ein sicheres Handling. Mit zwölf Stufen lässt sich die Vibrationsstärke individuellen Vorlieben anpassen – die Steuerung erfolgt über einen Bedienknopf am ovalen Ende des Vibrators. Der leistungsstarke, jedoch im Flüstermodus arbeitende Motor lässt sich mittels des integrierten Akkus wieder aufladen, zudem ist das Toy wasserdicht.

Specially developed for women, the vibrator has a cylindrical, elegant design that will appeal to users who appreciate aesthetic and durable lifestyle products. The handy size, textured silicone surface and rounded tip make for safe, comfortable handling. There are 12 settings for adapting the strength of the vibrations to individual preferences, selected via a control button at the oval end of the waterproof toy. The powerful but whisper-quiet motor is powered by an integrated rechargeable battery.

SPECIAL MENTION

KICKERLAND STECKKICKER

TISCHKICKER TABLE FOOTBALL

> **JURY STATEMENT**
>
> Der Werbe-Kicker ist überraschend gut bespielbar, trotz seiner kleinen Abmessungen. Das Produkt macht Spaß und fordert unmittelbar auf, es auszuprobieren.
>
> Despite its small dimensions, the promotional table football game is surprisingly good to play with. The product is fun and makes you want to try it out the minute you see it.

HERSTELLER/MANUFACTURER
b+a Vertriebs GmbH
Ilsfeld

DESIGN
Inhouse

VERTRIEB/DISTRIBUTOR
b+a Vertriebs GmbH
Ilsfeld

Zu mehreren spielbar und mit hohem Spaßfaktor – Tischkicker gehören zu den beliebtesten Spielgeräten. Das macht sie auch attraktiv für den Werbemittelmarkt. Der zusammensteckbare und individuell bedruckbare Tischkicker im Mini-Format geht hier neue Wege: Bestehen konventionelle Kicker dieser Größe aus fünf bis sieben unterschiedlichen Materialien, wurden hier ausschließlich Birken-Multiplexplatten verarbeitet. Die Wasserstrahl-Schneidtechnik erfordert lediglich einen mechanischen Arbeitsgang, und durch die fehlende Spielfläche können 40 Prozent Material eingespart werden. Außerdem belegt dieser Kicker, sollte er mal nicht bespielt werden, keinen Stauraum und lässt sich schnell und platzsparend zerlegen.

Suitable for multiple players, table football comes with a big fun factor and is an enduring favourite with games fans. That makes it attractive for the promotional merchandise market too. This slot-together, custom-printable version of the game in miniature format breaks new ground: whereas conventional specimens of this size consist of five to seven different materials, this one is made entirely from birch multiplex. The waterjet cutting technique means only one mechanical process is necessary, and the absence of a playing surface saves 40 percent in terms of the amount of material required. What's more, rather than taking up valuable storage space, the game is simply taken apart when not in use.

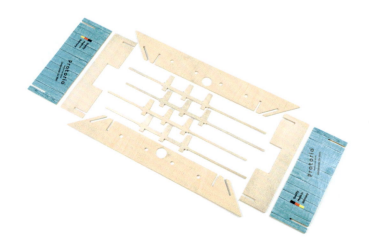

TILO WÜSTHOFF   **INDUSTRIAL DESIGN, GAUTING**

»Mittlerweile gibt es den Focus Open seit 30 Jahren. Das macht den Award aus meiner Sicht so interessant, relevant und auch international glaubwürdig.«

»Focus Open has been going for 30 years now. In my view, that's what makes the award so interesting and relevant, as well as giving it international credibility.«

Tilo Wüsthoff arbeitete nach seinem Universitätsabschluss in Industriedesign beim Deutschen Zentrum für Luft- und Raumfahrt und wirkte an verschiedenen Robotik- und Raumfahrtprojekten des DLR sowie der Europäischen Raumfahrtagentur (ESA) mit. Seit 2013 arbeitet er zudem mit seinem eigenen Büro für Hightech-Startups im Bereich der Robotik. Wüsthoff konzentriert sich stets darauf, nutzer*innenzentriertes Design und modernste Technologie miteinander zu verbinden.

www.tilo-wuesthoff.de

After graduating in industrial design, Tilo Wüsthoff worked at the German Aerospace Center and has been involved with various robotics and aerospace projects for both the German Aerospace Center (DLR) and the European Space Agency (ESA). In addition, he has been working for high-tech startups in the robotics industry on a freelance basis since 2013. Wüsthoff consistently focuses on combining user-centred design with state-of-the-art technology.

www.tilo-wuesthoff.de

1 → SEITE / PAGE
154–159

2 → SEITE / PAGE
160, 166

3 → SEITE / PAGE
161, 167

4 → SEITE / PAGE
162, 168

5 → SEITE / PAGE
163, 169

6 → SEITE / PAGE
164, 170

PUBLIC DESIGN, URBAN DESIGN

1	**GOLD:** **JÜDISCHES MUSEUM GÖPPINGEN** Stadt Göppingen Archiv und Museen Göppingen
2	**SILVER:** **STUTTGART IN DER VERLORENEN ZEIT** StadtPalais Stuttgart – Museum für Stuttgart Stuttgart
3	**WASSERWERTSCHÄTZEN** Wasserzweckverband Rottenburger Gruppe Rottenburg a. d. Laaber
4	**SPECIAL MENTION:** **PERSPEKTIVEN ZUR FREIHEIT** Landeszentrale für Politische Bildung Mecklenburg-Vorpommern Schwerin
5	**DRAUFGESETZT** Livable Cities GmbH Mannheim
6	**CL6720** Recaro Aircraft Seating GmbH & Co. KG Schwäbisch Hall

Gestaltung für die Öffentlichkeit ist immer auch von der Inszenierung geprägt – besonders Ausstellungskonzepte mit ihren multimedialen Präsentationen von Exponaten und Geschichten bedienen sich diesem Prinzip. Aber auch der öffentliche Raum gewinnt durch gestalterisch durchdachte Systeme an Attraktivität, Transparenz und Vielfalt.

Design for the public is always influenced by the need to stage things to some extent – exhibition concepts are particularly likely to adopt this principle in the form of multimedia exhibits and narratives. But well-designed systems add to the attractiveness, transparency and diversity of the public space too.

PUBLIC DESIGN, URBAN DESIGN
PUBLIC DESIGN, URBAN DESIGN

154
155

FOCUS GOLD

GOLD — JÜDISCHES MUSEUM GÖPPINGEN

AUSSTELLUNGSKONZEPTION / EXHIBITION CONCEPT

JURY STATEMENT

Allein schon die Kombination von Ort und Thema ist spannend. Die Ausstellung integriert sich sehr gut in den Kirchenraum und respektiert dessen eigene Rolle. Dennoch ist die Schau sehr prägnant gestaltet, sie zeigt sich sachlich mit gut gelöster, typografischer Ausarbeitung.

The combination of site and subject is intriguing in itself. The exhibition integrates with the interior of the church very well and respects the role it plays. Nevertheless, the new design is very striking, takes an objective approach and is enhanced by the accompanying typography.

AUFTRAGGEBER/CLIENT
Stadt Göppingen
Archiv und Museen Göppingen

DESIGN
Ranger Design Stuttgart
und/and
Karl-Heinz Rueß

Das Museum widmet sich der Geschichte der jüdischen Bevölkerung des Göppinger Teilortes Jebenhausen und fand bereits 1992 in der dortigen ehemaligen evangelischen Kirche seinen Platz. Präsentierte das Museum zunächst die Zeitspanne von 1777 bis zum Ende des Zweiten Weltkriegs, so steuert die Aktualisierung 2019 neue Erkenntnisse bei, widmet sich zusätzlich der Erinnerungskultur und wagt einen Blick in die Zukunft. Erstfassung und Update wurden vom gleichen Büro gestaltet. Das primär auf Wissensvermittlung ausgelegte Konzept geht behutsam mit der historischen Sakralarchitektur um, verdichtet und weitet sich, ähnelt einer zweiten, über der Bausubstanz liegenden Geschichtsebene.

Die Neugestaltung versteht sich als Weiterentwicklung, die vorhandenen Einbauten und Vitrinen wurden modifiziert und weitestgehend übernommen.

The museum is dedicated to the history of the Jewish population in Jebenhausen near Göppingen in Baden-Württemberg and was established in the village's former Protestant church in 1992. While the museum initially presented the period from 1777 until the end of World War II, the 2019 update contributes new insights, as well as addressing the culture of remembrance and venturing a look into the future. Both the original and new designs are the work of the same firm. Primarily designed for the communication of knowledge, the concept is mindful of the historical religious architecture, expands and contracts, like a second level of history lying over the fabric of the building.

The new design is conceived as an evolution, for the most part the existing fixtures and display cases were modified and reused.

KURT RANGER   **INHABER, RANGER DESIGN**

»Inhalt und Form bilden eine sich gegenseitig beeinflussende Einheit.«

»The content and form influence one another and combine to create a single entity.«

KURT RANGER
OWNER, RANGER DESIGN

→ **Ein jüdisches Museum in einer ehemaligen evangelischen Kirche ist ungewöhnlich. Hatte dies Auswirkungen auf Ihre Konzeption?**

Die räumliche Umgebung einer Ausstellung spielt eine große Rolle. Die alte Kirche von 1506 bildet das historische Ambiente für das eigentliche Thema der Ausstellung, die Geschichte der jüdischen Bevölkerung in Jebenhausen und Göppingen seit 1777. Meine Absicht war es, den Raumeindruck zu erhalten und respektvoll mit ihm umzugehen. Daraus entstand das Raumkonzept. Es bildet eine zweite Schicht, lässt Blickachsen und Freiräume offen und verdichtet an anderen Stellen. Und es hebt die Schenkungen der Jüdischen Gemeinde an die Kirche hervor.

Sie haben das Museum bereits 1992 gestaltet – wie schreibt man ein Konzept nach über zwei Jahrzehnten fort?

Eigentlich hätte das Design der 1990er-Jahre weiter funktioniert, da es keinen Gestaltungsmoden folgte. Den eigentlichen Impuls zur Neugestaltung gab die Forschung der letzten Jahrzehnte. Es war wichtig, sie in das neue Konzept einfließen zu lassen. 1992 stand der Holocaust am Ende der Ausstellung. Heute stehen die Begriffe »Anklagen, Erinnern, Gedenken, Begegnen« am Ende.

Warum wurde die Ausstellung nicht insgesamt neu konzipiert?

Das Raumkonzept hatte sich bewährt. Die Ausstellung wurde inhaltlich komplett neu durchdacht und neu gestaltet, auf der Basis vorhandener Raumstrukturen. Inhalt und Form bilden eine sich gegenseitig beeinflussende Einheit. Die Inhalte sind nicht grundsätzlich andere als Ende der 1980er-Jahre. Es kam vielmehr neues Wissen dazu. Der Holocaust spielt nach wie vor eine zentrale Rolle, aber auch die Begegnung mit der jüdischen Kultur.

Es gab keinen Grund, alle Unterkonstruktionen und Vitrinen zu entsorgen. Die Ausstellung wirkt komplett neu, ist aber nachhaltig.

Sie setzen vergleichsweise wenig multimediale Elemente ein – warum?

In den vergangenen acht Jahren haben wir drei Mal den Sinus Award für herausragende künstlerische Leistungen und Lösungen beim Einsatz von Technik in audiovisuellen Installationen erhalten: für das FC Bayern Museum, das Hilti Innovation Center und die World of Light von Osram. Trotzdem setzen wir Medien nur dort ein, wo sie inhaltlich Sinn machen. Im Jüdischen Museum gibt es derzeit fünf Medienstationen, eine weitere folgt. Das ist vollkommen ausreichend. Originales Filmmaterial gibt es nur ganz wenig. Trotzdem bewegt das Jüdische Museum Besuchende sehr.

Hinter Ranger Design steht ein Team aus erfahrenen Spezialisten um den Ausstellungsgestalter Kurt Ranger, das bisher über 150 Museen, Showrooms, Ausstellungen, Messestände und Erlebniswelten konzipiert hat. Das Spektrum der Aufgaben reicht von der Gestaltung von Zeitungen und Magazinen bis hin zu neuen Konzepten für die Stadtentwicklung.

www.ranger-design.com

→ **A Jewish museum in a former Protestant church is unusual. Did that have any impact on your concept?**

The physical surroundings of an exhibition play a major role. The old church from 1506 provides the historical ambience for the actual theme of the exhibition, the history of the Jewish population in Jebenhausen and Göppingen since 1777. My intention was to preserve the feel of the space and treat it with respect. That's what the concept grew out of. It forms a second layer, leaves sightlines and empty spaces open in some places and condenses in others. And it highlights the gifts the Jewish community made to the church.

You designed the museum when it first opened in 1992 – how do you take up a concept again after more than two decades?

The design from the 1990s would have continued to work because it didn't follow any particular fashions. The impetus for redesigning the museum actually came from the research that has taken place in recent decades. It was important to incorporate it in the new concept. In 1992, the exhibition ended with the Holocaust. Today it ends with a section entitled Accuse, Remember, Commemorate, Encounter.

Why wasn't the entire exhibition reimagined?

The spatial concept had proved itself. The content of the exhibition was completely rethought and redesigned on the basis of the existing spatial structures. The content and form influence one another and combine to create a single entity. The content isn't fundamentally different than in the late 1980s. It was more a case of new knowledge being added. The Holocaust continues to play a key role, but so does the encounter with the Jewish culture. There was no reason to get rid of all the substructures and display cases. The exhibition looks completely new, but it's sustainable.

You use relatively few multimedia elements – why?

Three times in the last eight years, we've received the Sinus Award for outstanding artistic achievements and solutions with respect to the use of technology in audiovisual installations: for the FC Bayern Museum, the Hilti Innovation Center and the Osram World of Light. Nevertheless, we only use media where it makes sense in relation to the content. There are currently five media stations in the Jewish Museum, with another set to follow. That's totally sufficient. Even though there's very little original film footage, the Jewish Museum is a very moving experience.

Ranger Design consists of a team of experienced specialists headed by exhibition designer Kurt Ranger and is responsible for the concepts behind more than 150 museums, showrooms, exhibitions, trade fair booths and leisure attractions. Its spectrum of work ranges from designing newspapers and magazines all the way to new concepts for urban development.

www.ranger-design.com

SILVER STUTTGART IN DER VERLORENEN ZEIT → SEITE / PAGE 166 TEMPORÄRE ESCAPE-AUSSTELLUNG TEMPORARY ESCAPE EXHIBITION

| SPECIAL MENTION | PERSPEKTIVEN ZUR FREIHEIT
→ SEITE / PAGE 168 | BEGEHBARE INSTALLATION
WALK-THROUGH INSTALLATION |

| SPECIAL MENTION | DRAUFGESETZT → SEITE / PAGE 169 | STADTMÖBEL STREET FURNITURE |

SPECIAL MENTION CL6720 FLUGZEUGSITZ / AIRCRAFT SEAT

→ SEITE / PAGE 170

164
165

SILVER

STUTTGART IN DER VERLORENEN ZEIT

TEMPORÄRE ESCAPE-AUSSTELLUNG / TEMPORARY ESCAPE EXHIBITION

> **JURY STATEMENT**
>
> Die Ausstellung ist mit sehr viel Liebe zum Detail gestaltet und bietet eine Menge kindgerechter Interaktionen sowie Entdeck-Momente. Dabei stehen virtuelle und haptisch erfahrbare Elemente in einem guten Verhältnis zueinander.
>
> The exhibition has been designed with great attention to detail and provides a wealth of child-friendly interaction and moments of discovery. It also succeeds in striking a good balance between virtual and physical elements.

Mit einem interaktiven Spielerlebnis und ganz neuen Formen der Vermittlung von Inhalten der Stuttgarter Stadtgeschichte spricht die Ausstellung vor allem junge Menschen und Familien mit Kindern an. In Anlehnung an das Prinzip des Escape-Rooms gilt es, auf einer fiktiven Zeitreise in die Vergangenheit Stuttgarts verschiedene Rätsel zu lösen und Missionen zu erfüllen. Ganz spielerisch werden so auf drei unterschiedlichen Zeitebenen geschichtliche Zusammenhänge erläutert und für die Besucher*innen sicht- und erlebbar.

Mainly aimed at young people and families with children, the exhibition features an interactive game experience and totally new approaches to imparting the history of Stuttgart. Based on the escape room principle, it invites visitors to solve mysteries and accomplish missions as they journey back in time through the city's past. The exhibition thus provides playful access to the historical contexts of three different eras, making them come to life in a way that visitors can see and experience for themselves.

AUFTRAGGEBER / CLIENT
StadtPalais Stuttgart –
Museum für Stuttgart
Stuttgart

DESIGN
Visuell Studio für
Kommunikation GmbH
Stuttgart

FOTOS / PHOTOS
Julia Ochs

SILVER

WASSERWERT-SCHÄTZEN

AUSSTELLUNGSKONZEPTION / EXHIBITION CONCEPT

JURY STATEMENT

Die Ausstellung folgt einem sehr klaren Konzept, bereitet das wichtige Thema Wasser verständlich auf, bleibt dabei aber eher auf der sachlichen Ebene. Verständliche Visualisierungen und eine gute Zugänglichkeit zu den Inhalten vermitteln Wissen mit Alltagsbezug.

The exhibition is based on a very clear concept and presents the important topic of water in a comprehensible way while remaining on an objective level. Straightforward visualisations and the accessibility of the content succeed in imparting knowledge that is relevant to visitors' everyday lives.

AUFTRAGGEBER / CLIENT
Wasserzweckverband
Rottenburger Gruppe
Rottenburg a. d. Laaber

DESIGN
Panoorama
München / Munich

Ganz auf junge Besucher konzentriert sich diese Ausstellung und vermittelt dieser Zielgruppe wichtiges Wissen über die wertvolle Ressource Wasser. Das passiert an 13 interaktiven und multimedialen Stationen mit unterschiedlichsten Exponaten aus dem Alltag. Die Dauerausstellung des Wasserversorgers arbeitet auch mit Texten, Infografiken, Fotos und Videos, um die teils komplexen Zusammenhänge der Wasserwirtschaft begreifbar zu machen – und um zu zeigen, dass die stetige Verfügbarkeit des Wassers nicht so selbstverständlich ist. Die teils spielerisch angelegten Inszenierungen steigern die Wertschätzung für sauberes Wasser.

Focused on young visitors, the exhibition aims to impart important knowledge about water and encourage this target group's perception of it as a valuable resource. It does so by means of 13 interactive and multimedia stations with all sorts of exhibits from everyday life. The water company's permanent exhibition also uses texts, infographics, photos and videos to make the sometimes complex topic of water supply and distribution tangible and accessible – and to show that the constant availability of water should by no means be taken for granted. The sometimes playfully designed presentations encourage youngsters to appreciate the value of clean water.

SPECIAL MENTION

PERSPEKTIVEN ZUR FREIHEIT

BEGEHBARE INSTALLATION
WALK-THROUGH INSTALLATION

JURY STATEMENT

Bemerkenswert, dass diese Installation nur auf Text beruht und dennoch so eindrücklich wirkt. Die Idee ist gestalterisch sehr sauber umgesetzt und wirkt nicht laut, sondern angenehm luftig.

It's remarkable that this installation is based solely on text and yet is so very impressive. The idea has been translated into a very crisp design that is anything but loud and conjures a pleasantly airy feel.

AUFTRAGGEBER/CLIENT
Landeszentrale für Politische Bildung Mecklenburg-Vorpommern
Schwerin

DESIGN
Dagmar Korintenberg & Wolf Kipper
Stuttgart

Die friedlichen Demonstrationen und die Ereignisse im Herbst 1989, die schließlich zur Wiedervereinigung Deutschlands führten, sind fest im kollektiven Gedächtnis verankert. Die Installation auf dem Vorplatz der Warener St. Georgen Kirche in Mecklenburg-Vorpommern erinnert 30 Jahre später daran, für welche Werte die Demonstrant*innen damals auf die Straße gingen: Demokratie, Meinungsfreiheit, Frieden. Hohe Stützen tragen Metall-Banner, in denen die Losungen jener Zeit ausgelasert und gegen den Himmel lesbar sind. Eine AR-Anwendung vermittelt zudem Zugang zu dokumentarischen Filmaufnahmen und Fotos von Zeitzeug*innen.

The peaceful demonstrations and events of autumn 1989 that eventually led to the reunification of Germany are firmly anchored in the country's collective memory. Today, 30 years later, the installation on the forecourt of St George's church in Waren, Mecklenburg-Vorpommern, is a reminder of the values that the demonstrators took to the streets for: democracy, freedom of speech, peace. Long poles support metal banners with the slogans of those days lasered out of them so that they can be read against the sky. In addition, an AR app provides access to documentary film footage and photos of those who were there.

SPECIAL MENTION — DRAUFGESETZT — STADTMÖBEL / STREET FURNITURE

JURY STATEMENT

Der öffentliche Raum wird derzeit neu entdeckt, besonders in urbanen Zentren. Mit den modularen, schnell installierten Möbeln lassen sich neue Angebote zur Aneignung auch kleiner Ecken einfach realisieren. Ein Zugewinn an Lebensqualität!

The public space is being rediscovered, especially in urban centres. The modular furniture is quick and simple to install and creates new options so that people can make even the smallest corner their own. A great way to enhance quality of life in the city!

HERSTELLER / MANUFACTURER
Livable Cities GmbH
Mannheim

DESIGN
Inhouse

VERTRIEB / DISTRIBUTOR
Livable Cities GmbH
Mannheim

Städte sind dann lebenswerte Orte, wenn sie ausreichend große und qualitativ hochwertige Möglichkeiten für den Aufenthalt und die Begegnung von Menschen bieten. Sich im Freien niederzulassen, ist beliebt – hier setzt das flexible Möblierungssystem an und bietet im urbanen Leben eine Alternative zur monofunktionalen, langweiligen Sitzbank. Die einzelnen, passgenau kombinierbaren Bankmodule lassen sich durch Add-Ons in Form von Tischen, Mülleimern, Anzeigetafeln oder autarken Lademöglichkeiten beliebig erweitern. Produziert wird regional in Baden-Württemberg, das robuste Holz stammt von der Pfälzer Edelkastanie.

Cities are liveable when they provide sufficiently large and high-quality options for people who want to spend time and meet others outdoors. Sitting in the fresh air is popular – and that's the starting point for this flexible furnishing system, which enhances urban living with an alternative to the boring, monofunctional bench. The individual bench modules fit together perfectly when combined and can be extended as required thanks to add-ons in the form of tables, litter bins, display boards or self-sufficient charging options. Produced regionally in Baden-Württemberg, the wooden furniture is made of robust local chestnut.

SPECIAL MENTION　　CL6720　　FLUGZEUGSITZ / AIRCRAFT SEAT

JURY STATEMENT

Flugzeugsitze zeigen immer wieder, dass trotz strikter Vorgaben bezüglich Gewicht oder Größe sehr bequeme, nutzerfreundliche und formal überzeugende Lösungen entstehen können. Das gilt für diesen Langstreckensitz ganz besonders.

Again and again, aircraft seats demonstrate that it's possible to create very comfortable, user-friendly and compellingly designed solutions despite the strict requirements governing their weight or size. This long-haul seat is a particularly convincing example.

HERSTELLER / MANUFACTURER
Recaro Aircraft Seating
GmbH & Co. KG
Schwäbisch Hall

DESIGN
Inhouse

VERTRIEB / DISTRIBUTOR
Recaro Aircraft Seating
GmbH & Co. KG
Schwäbisch Hall

Entwickelt wurde der Sitz für Reisende der Business Class, die auf Langstrecken unterwegs sind. Dafür bietet der Sitz nicht nur viel Privatsphäre und Stauraum, sondern auch unterschiedliche Sitzpositionen, die über eine Konsole abrufbar und individuell anpassbar sind. So lässt sich der Sitz in eine ebene Liegefläche verwandeln, die trotz eines Sitzteilers von nur 1,06 Metern volle 1,98 Meter lang ist. Auf diese Weise bringt der Sitz den Komfort der First Class in die Business Class – bei maximaler Raumeffizienz. Dank der geringen Sitzabstände finden so im Businessabteil eines Langstrecken-Jets rund 30 Sitze Platz. Mit 85 Kilogramm Gewicht ist der Sitz der leichteste seiner Art, er kann zudem selbst eine Funktionsdiagnose durchführen und lässt sich kabellos warten. Eine App ermöglicht es Reisenden, ihre bevorzugte Licht- und Sitzsituation abzuspeichern.

The seat was developed for business class passengers on long-haul flights. Besides providing ample privacy and storage space, the seat also permits various positions that can be accessed and individually adjusted via a console. It can also be transformed into a flat surface that is a full 1.98 metres long, despite a seat pitch of just 1.06 metres. As a result, it brings first-class comfort to business class while ensuring maximum space efficiency. Thanks to the short distances between individual seats, the business cabin of a long-haul jet can accommodate around 30 of them. Weighing in at 85 kilograms, the seat is the lightest of its kind; what's more, it can perform its own diagnostic check and is designed for wireless maintenance. An app enables passengers to save their preferred settings for the lighting and seat position.

SVEN VON BOETTICHER **ID AID, STUTTGART**

»Die Gestaltung von Produkten wird immer anspruchsvoller und vielfältiger. Alle Dinge werden intelligenter, kommunizieren mit uns, sind in Systeme eingebunden und können in Zukunft noch viel, viel mehr. Was wir uns heute ausdenken, wird zur Wirklichkeit von morgen.«

»Designing products is becoming an increasingly challenging and multifaceted profession. All the things around us are becoming more intelligent and communicating with us, they're integrated into systems and will be able to do much, much more in future. What we think up today becomes tomorrow's reality.«

Sven von Boetticher studierte Industriedesign an der Staatlichen Akademie der Bildenden Künste in Stuttgart. Um den Lebensraum des Menschen umfassend und komplex zu gestalten, arbeitet er nicht nur als Designer, sondern auch in den Bereichen Architektur und Interior-Design. 2011 gründete er das Designstudio ID AID in Stuttgart mit Schwerpunkt auf Produktgestaltung, Designkonzept und Markenarchitektur. Dabei geht es ihm immer darum, Leidenschaft mit Qualität und Innovation mit Nachhaltigkeit zu verbinden.

www.idaid.com

Sven von Boetticher studied industrial design at Stuttgart State Academy of Art and Design (ABK Stuttgart). In order to design people's living space with the necessary completeness and complexity, he is active not just as a designer but in the fields of architecture and interior design as well. In 2011 he founded the ID AID design studio in Stuttgart, which focuses on product design, design concepts and brand architecture. For him, it's always about combining passion with quality and innovation with sustainability.

www.idaid.com

1 → SEITE / PAGE 176–181

2 → SEITE / PAGE 182–187

3 → SEITE / PAGE 188, 192

4 → SEITE / PAGE 189, 193

5 → SEITE / PAGE 190, 194

MOBILITY
MOBILITY

GOLD:
1 **MEGA MACS X**
   Hella Gutmann Solutions GmbH
   Ihringen

2 **MONTEREY 5 IST**
   FIXSAFE I-SIZE
   Diono LLC
   Sumner, USA

SILVER:
3 **REGINUS**
   SKA Sitze GmbH
   Wörth am Rhein

SPECIAL MENTION:
4 **DAYTONA MOTO UPGRADE**
   Daytona Corporation
   Shizuoka, Japan

5 **PELIKAN**
   Rupert Kopp Product Design
   Berlin

Die Mobilität ist ein Schlüsselthema der Moderne – und eines, das vor großen Transformationen steht. Zugleich diversifizieren sich die Mobilitätsangebote immer weiter, einschließlich spezifischer Detaillösungen für Services, Wartung oder Individualisierung. Mobility bleibt spannend.

Mobility is a key theme of the modern age – and one that is facing major transformations. At the same time, mobility offerings are becoming increasingly diversified, including specific detail solutions for services, maintenance or customisation. Mobility remains a fascinating field.

12

GOLD | MEGA MACS X | FAHRZEUG-DIAGNOSEGERÄT
AUTOMOTIVE DIAGNOSTIC DEVICE

FOCUS
GOLD

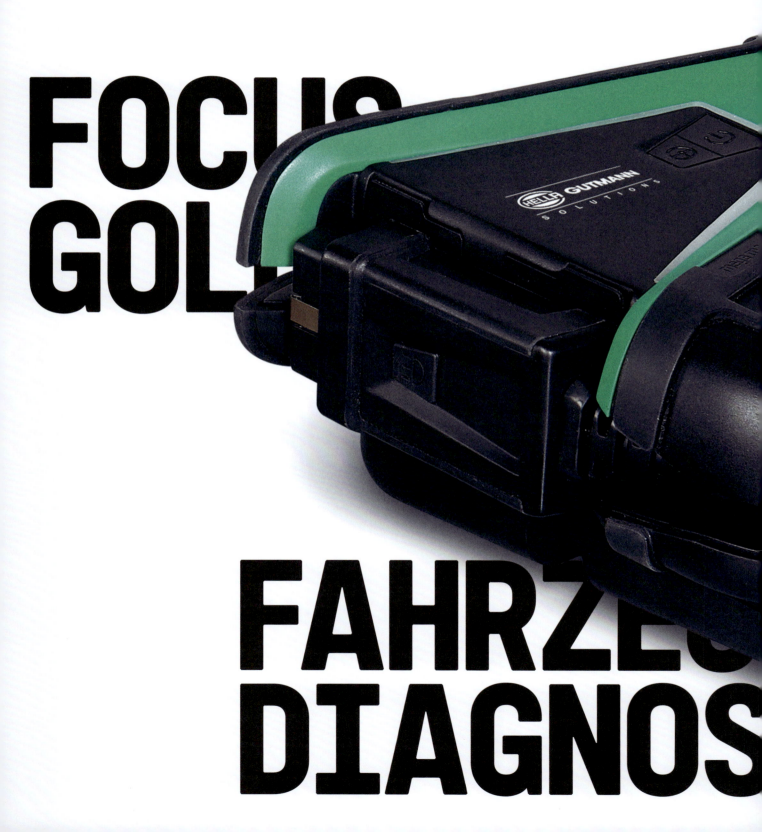

FAHRZEUG
DIAGNOSE

MEGA MACS X

GERÄT

GOLD — MEGA MACS X — FAHRZEUG-DIAGNOSEGERÄT / AUTOMOTIVE DIAGNOSTIC DEVICE

JURY STATEMENT

Hier schlägt das Herz des Industriedesigners höher – alle Funktionen und Details sind bestens durchdacht. Das meist vernachlässigte Kabelmanagement ist eindeutig gelöst, das induktive Laden wird über die Formgebung unterstützt, auch Details stimmen. So erleichtern LEDs im Stecker das Auffinden der Diagnosebuchse im Fußraum.

The device is enough to warm an industrial designer's heart: all the functions and details have been meticulously thought through. A straightforward solution has been found for the often-neglected cable management dilemma, the design facilitates the inductive charging process, every detail is meaningful. The LEDs in the connector, for example, help locate the diagnostic socket in the car's footwell.

HERSTELLER/MANUFACTURER
Hella Gutmann Solutions GmbH
Ihringen

DESIGN
Defortec GmbH
Dettenhausen

VERTRIEB/DISTRIBUTOR
Hella Gutmann Solutions GmbH
Ihringen

Speziell für markenunabhängige Werkstätten gedacht, liest dieses Diagnosegerät die Daten von Fahrzeugen unterschiedlichster Hersteller aus. Um im rauen Reparaturalltag bestehen zu können, ist das Gehäuse sturzresistent ausgelegt – seine verstärkten Ecken visualisieren diese Robustheit. Die Konzeption folgt einer klaren Nutzungsorientierung: So kann das Kabel mit dem Diagnosestecker in einer umlaufenden Nut aufgerollt werden, der Stecker selbst wird per integriertem Magnet sicher und geschützt fixiert. Grüne Lichtlaufbalken im Gehäuse signalisieren den Mitarbeiter*innen in der Werkstatt den laufenden Datenverkehr. Mittels eines großen, rückseitigen Hakenelements kann das Gerät an der halb geöffneten Seitenscheibe des Fahrzeuges eingehängt werden – diese Positionierung verbessert den drahtlosen Datenaustausch zum Notebook oder Tablet, das die eigentliche Diagnose übernimmt.

Designed with independent workshops in mind, this diagnostic device can read the data from vehicles by a wide range of manufacturers. The impact-resistant housing is made to withstand the tough everyday conditions in a garage environment and features reinforced corners that visualise its robustness. The concept centres on the usage scenario: the cable with the diagnostic connector is coiled into a groove around the circumference of the device, for instance, and the connector itself is held in place by an integrated magnet for extra protection. Scrolling green lights in the housing signal to workshop staff that the data transmission is in progress. A large hook element on the back of the device is used to hang it from the vehicle's half-open side window – a position that improves the wireless connection with the paired notebook or tablet that performs the actual diagnosis.

ILJA KLOBERTANZ UND LIONEL LINKE INDUSTRIEDESIGNER, DEFORTEC GMBH

»Genau genommen entwickelten wir die Form aus den Usability-Anforderungen heraus.«

»Strictly speaking, we developed the form out of the usability requirements.«

links / left: Lionel Linke
rechts / right: Ilja Klobertanz

ILJA KLOBERTANZ AND LIONEL LINKE
INDUSTRIAL DESIGNERS, DEFORTEC GMBH

→ Mit welchen Vorgaben sind Sie in die Entwicklung gegangen?

Da es sich um ein Profitool handelt, haben wir uns zuerst angeschaut, wie die Arbeit in den Werkstätten abläuft. Dadurch konnten wir die Anforderungen an Robustheit, Langlebigkeit, Handling und Usability nutzungsgerecht lösen. Das Gerät sollte so klein wie möglich werden, zusammen mit den Elektronikern des Herstellers konnten wir das Packaging der Komponenten optimieren. Ein ganz wichtiger Punkt war für uns das Kabelmanagement. Gerade Kabel werden oft sich selbst überlassen und bei der Gestaltung vernachlässigt. Daher lässt sich das 1,5 Meter lange Diagnosekabel nun zwischen den beiden Gehäuseschalen aufwickeln. Und der Stecker hat einen geschützten Ruheplatz mit magnetischer Fixierung.

Das hört sich sehr funktional gedacht an, wo bleibt da die Gestaltung?

Natürlich sollte das Tool auch ästhetisch zur Zielgruppe passen, daher haben wir bewusst Designelemente aus dem automotiven Bereich integriert – zum Beispiel die dynamische Lichtsignatur, die zugleich als Status-Anzeige dient. Außerdem haben wir Designelemente entwickelt, die sich auf weitere Geräte übertragen ließen.

Welche Relevanz hatte die Usability?

Eine ganz große. Genau genommen entwickelten wir die Form aus den Usability-Anforderungen heraus, die Verrundungen steigern die Robustheit, die Zweiteilung sorgt für das Kabelmanagement, sachte Rücksprünge machen das Gehäuse griffiger und die wenigen Tasten sind fehlertolerant vertieft integriert. Der Seitenscheiben-Fixierungshaken dient zugleich der eindeutigen Positionierung in der formal gleich gestalteten Ladebasis.

Das langlebige Tool muss leicht zu reparieren sein – was hat das Design dazu beigetragen?

Wir haben zunächst die Platzierung der Komponenten optimiert – in der einen Schale des asymmetrischen Gehäuses befindet sich der Akku, in der anderen die elektronischen Komponenten. Dank gut zugänglicher Verschraubungspunkte kommt man schnell und direkt an das Innere. Die Trennfuge der Schalen befindet sich in der Kabelnut, ist also nicht sichtbar. Übrigens haben wir auch die Öffnungen für die aktive Kühlung in die Nut gelegt, denn die wird ja bei aufgewickeltem Kabel nicht benötigt. Um all das umzusetzen, muss man schlussendlich die gesamte Technik des Gerätes gut verstehen.

Defortec ist auf die Entwicklung und Gestaltung komplexer technischer Produkte spezialisiert, Großanlagen inklusive. Das Büro wurde 2011 von Stefan Grobe gegründet, ist international aktiv und wiederholt beim Focus Open mit Gold-Preisen ausgezeichnet worden.

www.defortec.de

→ What guidelines did you have when you started on the development?

Because the tool is meant for professional use, the first thing we did was to take a look at the routines and processes in workshops. That enabled us to come up with solutions that were fit for purpose in terms of robustness, durability, handling and usability. We were asked to make the device as small as possible, and together with the manufacturer's electronic engineers we were able to optimise the packaging of the components. We viewed the cable management as a really important point. Cables are often left to themselves and neglected by the design. That's why we came up with the solution of coiling the 1.5-metre-long diagnostic cable between the two shells of the housing. And the connector is protected when not in use because it's kept in place by a magnetic holder.

That sounds like a very functional approach, where does that leave the design side of things?

Obviously the tool should have an aesthetic in keeping with the target group, so we deliberately integrated design elements from the automotive sector – like the dynamic light signature that doubles as a status indicator. We also developed certain design elements that could be transferred to other devices.

How relevant was usability?

It was an extremely important aspect. Strictly speaking, we developed the form out of the usability requirements: the rounded shapes make the device more robust, its division into two parts takes care of cable management, the recesses make the housing easier to grip and the few buttons are error-tolerant because they're set quite deep. The bracket for attaching the device to the side window of the car also ensures it's docked into the charging base in the correct position, because the charger is designed to accommodate it.

The made-to-last tool has to be easy to repair – what does the design contribute in that respect?

First, we optimised the position of the components – one shell of the asymmetric housing contains the battery, the other the electronic components. Thanks to the easily accessible screws, you can open it quickly and get straight to the inner workings. The join between the shells is inside the groove for the cable, so it's invisible. And by the way: we put the openings for active cooling in the groove too, because they're not needed when the cable is coiled up. At the end of the day, you can only implement all that if you have a good understanding of the entire technology behind the device.

Defortec specialises in the development and design of complex technical products, including large-scale plant. Founded in 2011 by Stefan Grobe, the agency is internationally active and has won multiple Focus Open Gold awards over the years.

www.defortec.de

GOLD

MONTEREY 5 IST FIXSAFE I-SIZE
AUTO-KINDERSITZ / CHILD CAR SEAT

JURY STATEMENT

Dem Design gelingt es vorzüglich, kindgerechte Gestaltung mit den ästhetischen Vorgaben von Fahrzeuginterieurs zu verbinden. Besonders herausragend ist die Faltfunktion, die den Sitz erheblich verkleinert, wenn er gerade nicht in Gebrauch ist. Bemerkenswert auch, dass all dies mit reduziertem Materialeinsatz einhergeht.

The designers have done an excellent job of combining child-friendly aspects with the aesthetic requirements of vehicle interiors. The folding function that makes the seat considerably smaller when not in use is particularly outstanding. It is also remarkable that all this has been achieved while simultaneously reducing the amount of materials used.

HERSTELLER/MANUFACTURER
Diono LLC
Sumner
USA

DESIGN
White ID GmbH & Co. KG
Schorndorf

VERTRIEB/DISTRIBUTOR
Diono UK Ltd
Manchester
Vereinigtes Königreich/
United Kingdom

Über ganze acht Jahre hinweg kann dieser Sitz Kinder bei Autofahrten begleiten und gemäß den neuesten europäischen Sicherheitsstandards schützen. Die Anpassung erfolgt über eine einfache, synchronisierte Höhen- und Breitenverstellung. Obwohl er besonders geräumig und komfortabel daherkommt, ist der Sitz auf kompaktes Handling ausgelegt. So lässt er sich für die Mitnahme außerhalb des Autos dank integrierter Faltfunktion auf ein Volumen von 78 Litern komprimieren und damit auch praktisch in Gepäckfächern verstauen. Ein Handgriff genügt und der Sitz ist wieder für die Nutzung bereit. Zudem reduziert die Faltfunktion den Verpackungsaufwand um ein Kilogramm und das Volumen um 40 Liter – ein äußerst positiver Nebeneffekt für die Logistik des Herstellers. Darüber hinaus spart die Konzeption zwei Kilogramm Material, das sich zudem sortenrein trennen lässt.

This seat can accompany children on car journeys for an entire eight years and provides protection that complies with the latest European safety standards. A simple synchronised mechanism adjusts the height and width of the seat to its growing user. Although it looks particularly roomy and comfortable, the seat is in fact designed for compactness to ensure maximum portability. Thanks to an integrated folding function, for instance, it can be compressed down to a volume of 78 litres for transport outside the car, enabling it to be conveniently stowed in overhead lockers. And once it's needed again, it takes just one simple step and the seat is ready to use. In addition, the folding function reduces the amount of packaging required by 1 kilogram and the volume by 40 litres – an extremely positive side effect for the manufacturer's logistics. What's more, the concept saves 2 kilograms of materials, and the product can later be separated into mono-materials for recycling.

ANDREAS HESS — MANAGING PARTNER, WHITE ID GMBH & CO. KG

»Handhabung und Bedienung eines Kinderrückhaltesystems sollten logisch und einfach sein.«

»The handling and use of a child restraint system should be logical and straightforward.«

links / left: Andreas Hess
rechts / right: Sebastian Schnabel

ANDREAS HESS
MANAGING PARTNER, WHITE ID GMBH & CO. KG

→ **Sie waren nicht nur für das Design, sondern für die komplette Konzeption des Kindersitzes zuständig. Wie komplex war die Entwicklung?**

Die große Herausforderung bei diesem Projekt bestand darin, aus dem sehr offenen und allgemeinen Briefing mit der Bezeichnung »Kinderrückhaltesystem für die Mobilität der Zukunft« ein Produkt zu entwickeln, das den Übergang von der heutigen Mobilität zu jener in fünf bis zehn Jahren begleitet. Wir mussten einerseits das gelernte Mobilitätsverhalten mit den absehbaren Veränderungen, also häufigere Wechsel zwischen den Verkehrsmitteln und mehr Flexibilität, in ein Produkt integrieren. Darüber hinaus galt es, Einfachheit, Sicherheit, Platzeffizienz, Trennbarkeit von Materialien und die Rahmenbedingungen des Onlinevertriebs zu berücksichtigen. Einige dieser Anforderungen widersprechen sich durchaus, haben aber das Projekt spannend und anspruchsvoll gemacht.

Sicherheit gehört zu den wichtigsten Anforderungen an einen Kindersitz – hat dies Einfluss auf das Design?

Ja, natürlich. Die Anforderungen durch Normen, Sicherheitsprüfungen und Tests beeinflussen die Entwicklung eines Kinderrückhaltesystems enorm. Im Idealfall zeigt sich das aber nur durch eine Gestaltung, die Vertrauen, Sicherheit und Komfort visualisiert und die technischen Notwendigkeiten von den Nutzer*innen fernhält. Denn sowohl Handhabung als auch Bedienung eines Kinderrückhaltesystems sollten logisch und einfach sein, um Fehler mit potenziell gravierenden Folgen zu vermeiden.

Was treibt die Entwicklung neuer Kindersitze generell an?

Der Wandel in der Mobilität ist hier sicher der wichtigste Treiber, aber auch Änderungen im Bereich der Sicherheitsnormen sind unbedingt zu nennen. Und nicht zu vergessen verändert sich ja auch das Nutzer*innenverhalten abseits der Mobilität. Das heißt, wir recherchieren auch, was Familien bewegt, wie ihr Selbstbild ist und über welche Produkte Werte kommuniziert werden.

Geht man Produkte für Kinder anders an?

Der Entwicklungsprozess unterscheidet sich kaum von anderen Produkten. Genaues Beobachten und Verstehen der Prozessschritte eines Produktes und der Nutzenden, fundiertes technisches Verständnis, ein kreativer und emotionaler Gestaltungsansatz und die Berücksichtigung von Herstellungsprozessen, Materialien und Normen sind wichtige Aspekte. Und das bei allen Projekten, die wir bearbeiten.

White ID wurde vor rund 20 Jahren gegründet – heute leiten Andreas Hess und Sebastian Schnabel das Unternehmen mit seinen zehn Mitarbeiter*innen. White ID – ID steht für Integrated Design – konzipiert unterschiedlichste Produkttypen. Ein Schwerpunkt sind aber Produkte für die Mobilität, etwa Kindersitze, Babytragen oder Kinderwagen.

www.white-id.com

→ **You were responsible not just for the design of the child seat but for the entire concept as well. How complex was the development?**

The major challenge with this project was to start from the very open-ended, general brief, which was simply described as »a child restraint system for the mobility of the future«, and develop a product that will accompany the transition from today's mobility to what we can expect in five to 10 years from now. On the one hand, we had to integrate learned mobility behaviour with the foreseeable changes, i.e. more frequent changes between different forms of transport and more flexibility, and combine both in one product. But it was also a case of considering aspects like simplicity, safety, an efficient use of space, the separability of the materials and the basic circumstances associated with online sales. Although some of those requirements are definitely contradictory, they made the project intriguing and challenging.

Safety is one of the most important requirements for a child seat – does that influence the design?

Yes, of course. The requirements resulting from the various standards, safety regulations and tests have a huge influence on the development of a child restraint system. Ideally, however, that's only apparent because you come up with a design that visualises trust, safety and comfort rather than confronting the user with the technical necessities head on. Because ultimately, both the handling and use of a child restraint system should be logical and straightforward so as to avoid mistakes with potentially serious consequences.

What drives the development of new child seats in a general sense?

The mobility transformation is definitely the most important driver, but changing safety standards are another crucial aspect. And it's important to remember that users' behaviour is changing in ways that aren't directly related to mobility too. So we also do research into what matters to families, how they see themselves and which products values are communicated by.

Do you take a different approach when you're dealing with products for children?

The development process is hardly any different from other products. Precise observation and understanding of the process stages that a product and its users go through, sound technical knowledge, a creative and emotional design approach and careful consideration of the manufacturing processes, materials and standards are all important aspects. And that applies to all the projects we work on.

White ID – ID stands for Integrated Design – was founded around 20 years ago. Today the company is headed by Andreas Hess and Sebastian Schnabel and employs a staff of 10. Although White ID develops a wide range of very different product types, mobility products such as child car seats, baby carriers and pushchairs are a key focus.

www.white-id.com

SILVER REGINUS SITZSYSTEM FÜR NAHVERKEHR
→ SEITE / PAGE SEATING SYSTEM FOR LOCAL TRANSPORT
192

| SPECIAL MENTION | DAYTONA MOTO UPGRADE → SEITE / PAGE 193 | MOTORRAD-KOMPONENTEN MOTORCYCLE COMPONENTS |

| SPECIAL MENTION | PELIKAN → SEITE / PAGE 194 | ELEKTROROLLER ELECTRIC SCOOTER |

SILVER

REGINUS

SITZSYSTEM FÜR NAHVERKEHR
SEATING SYSTEM FOR LOCAL TRANSPORT

JURY STATEMENT

Ein interessantes Konzept, sehr sauber gestaltet und modular gedacht. Es verbindet Sitzkomfort mit einer filigranen Anmutung und lässt sich ideal individualisieren. Dass dabei Holz eine zentrale Rolle spielt, unterstreicht den eigenständigen Ansatz.

An interesting concept with a very crisp design and modular approach. The seating combines comfort with slenderness and is ideal for customising. The fact that wood plays a key role underscores the originality of the design.

HERSTELLER/MANUFACTURER
SKA Sitze GmbH
Wörth am Rhein

DESIGN
Panik Ebner Design
Stuttgart

VERTRIEB/DISTRIBUTOR
SKA Sitze GmbH
Wörth am Rhein

Dieses System basiert auf separaten Sitz- und Rückenschalen, die über zwei Holme miteinander verbunden sind. Die Trennung von tragender Struktur und Schalen sorgt für eine freiere Gestaltung der Sitzkontur und ermöglicht den schnellen Austausch der Elemente bei Verschleiß oder Schaden. Zugleich lassen sich die Sitze mittels Polsterung, Oberflächen, Farben oder Funktionen modular anpassen. Die Sitze bieten einen verstärkten Seitenhalt, verschiedene Rückenlängen und Sitzbreiten sowie beispielsweise Klappoptionen. Sowohl Schalen als auch die tragenden Holme bestehen aus Holz.

Dank der ausgeprägten Individualisierbarkeit unterstützt das System die Differenzierung der ÖPNV-Angebote einzelner Betreiber.

The system is based on separate seat and back shells that are connected by two spars. The separation of the supporting structure and shells ensures greater freedom for designing the contours of the seat and simplifies the replacement of individual elements when they become worn or damaged. At the same time, the seats can be adjusted on a modular basis via the upholstery, surfaces, colours or functions. They provide greater lateral support than usual and are available with various back lengths, seat widths and additional features, including folding options. Both the shells and structural spars are made of wood.

Because it permits a high degree of customisation, the system can be used to distinguish between the offerings of different local public transport operators.

SPECIAL MENTION — DAYTONA MOTO UPGRADE — MOTORRAD-KOMPONENTEN / MOTORCYCLE COMPONENTS

JURY STATEMENT

Das ist eine sehr kluge Lösung, um Motorräder stilgerecht zu individualisieren. Alle Einzelelemente des Sets sind technisch und optisch aufeinander abgestimmt, die Gestaltung ist im klassischen Stil bewusst zurückgenommen.

A very clever solution for customising motorcycles in keeping with their original style. The technology and appearance of all the individual elements are geared to one another, and the design – in true classic fashion – is deliberately understated.

HERSTELLER / MANUFACTURER
Daytona Corporation
Shizuoka
Japan

DESIGN
Inhouse
Nikolaus Tams, Bernd Huth

VERTRIEB / DISTRIBUTOR
Daytona Europe
Hannover / Hanover

Wer seinem Motorrad einen klassischen Look verleihen möchte, muss nicht auf moderne Technik verzichten. So verbinden die Komponenten des Retro-Kits die LED-Technologie mit einer runden, reduzierten Formensprache, wie sie für alte Motorräder charakteristisch ist. Das Set besteht aus einem Hauptscheinwerfer sowie Front- und Heckblinkern, die zugleich die Funktion von Rück- und Bremslicht übernehmen – und ein optisch aufgeräumtes Heck ergeben. Ebenfalls klassisch gerundet präsentiert sich das 80 Millimeter große Kombi-Instrument mit analoger Zeigerdarstellung von Geschwindigkeit und Drehzahl, digitaler Kilometeranzeige und Kontrollanzeigen. Sowohl Instrument als auch Schweinwerfer lassen sich vielfältig montieren. Zudem verfügen alle Komponenten über die Europäischen Zulassungsnormen.

Giving your motorcycle a classic look doesn't mean you have to forgo modern technology. The components of this retro kit, for instance, combine LED technology with the kind of round, minimalist design language that's characteristic of old motorbikes. The set consists of a main headlight and front and rear indicators, the latter of which double as tail and brake lights, resulting in a pleasantly uncluttered rear view. The same round, classic form has been used for the combined gauge, which has analogue needles for speed and revs but a digital odometer and symbols. Both the gauge and the headlamp can be mounted in a variety of ways and all the components comply with European road-legal standards.

SPECIAL MENTION PELIKAN ELEKTROROLLER / ELECTRIC SCOOTER

> **JURY STATEMENT**
>
> Da stecken ganz viele gute Ideen für die urbane Mobilität drin, der Roller kann mit seinem universellen Ansatz eine aktuelle Lücke ausfüllen. Das Design ist pragmatisch angegangen und bietet viele Variationsoptionen. Interessant: Die Entwicklung startete ohne konkreten Auftraggeber.
>
> A whole lot of good ideas for urban mobility have gone into this scooter, which can fill a current gap with its universal approach. The design is pragmatic and provides plenty of options for variations. It's interesting to note that its development began with no specific client in mind.

HERSTELLER / MANUFACTURER
Rupert Kopp Product Design
Berlin

DESIGN
Rupert Kopp Product Design
Berlin

Das Konzept Pelikan ist sowohl Elektroroller als auch Plattform für unterschiedlichste Use Cases – das Fahrzeug ist universell gedacht und bietet daher eine Vielzahl an Andockpunkten für Transporthilfen, Behältnisse oder Zusatzsitze. Damit dieses Potenzial maximal genutzt werden kann, sind die Daten der Andockelemente und -bereiche frei verfügbar, die Aneignung und Individualisierung ist Teil des Produkts. Zur temporären Fixierung stehen unter anderem Zurrpunkte bereit, die sich als Plug-System aus den Oberflächen entnehmen lassen. Für den Antrieb sorgt ein Nabenmotor im Hinterrad, die Batterien befinden sich im Chassis aus Aluminium-Druckguss. Entwickelt wurde der bewusst einfach gehaltene und damit auch leicht reparierbare Roller für urbane Lieferdienste, Transportservices oder Leihsysteme.

The Pelikan concept is both an electric scooter and a platform for wide-ranging use cases – because it's intended to be universally usable, the vehicle provides a multitude of docking points for transport aids, containers or additional seats. To ensure this potential can be put to maximum use, the data relating to the dock-on elements and areas is freely available: appropriation and customisation are part of the product. The options for temporary attachment include lashing points, implemented in the form of a system of plugs that can be taken out of the surfaces. The scooter is powered by a hub motor in its rear wheel, the batteries are located in the die-cast aluminium chassis. Deliberately simple and therefore easy to repair, it was developed for urban delivery and transport services or sharing systems.

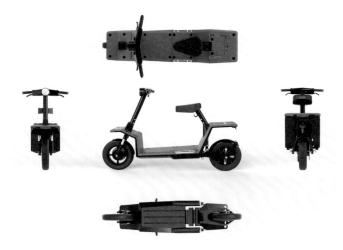

DR.-ING. SYBS BAUER MA (RCA) — **DESIGNKUNST, HAMBURG**

»Design hat auch die Aufgabe, zukunftsfähig, ökologisch und naturgerecht zu gestalten. Eine Verantwortung, die Designer*innen mit viel Zukunftswissen tragen können und sie verbinden in einer holistischen Haltung mit Liebe zum Detail verschiedene Disziplinen.«

»Part of design's job is to create things that are future-proof, ecological and compatible with nature. That's a responsibility that designers can take on because they have a good knowledge of what's coming in the future, plus they combine various disciplines within a holistic approach and have a passion for detail.«

Die diplomierte Industriedesignerin Dr. Sybs Bauer war einst Stipendiatin des Design Center Stuttgart (und des DAAD) für ihr Studium am Royal College of Art (UK) und promovierte berufsbegleitend 2019 an der TU München. 1996 gründete sie die Agentur designkunst in Caracas (VEN) und 2000 in Hamburg. Als Gastprofessorin lehrte und lehrt sie an internationalen Universitäten unter anderem an der Strate-School of Design, Paris, an der Duoc UC, Chile, und an der Bauhaus-Universität Weimar. Sie ist Vorsitzende der VDID Gruppe Nord und seit 2005 als Gender-Expertin Gutachterin für Femtech in Österreich.

www.designkunst.com

Industrial designer Dr Sybs Bauer studied at the Royal College of Art (UK) on a scholarship from the Design Center Stuttgart (and DAAD – the German Academic Exchange Service) and obtained her doctorate at TU Munich in 2019 as a part-time postgraduate. She founded the designkunst agency in Caracas (VEN) in 1996 and in Hamburg in 2000. She has taught as a visiting professor at various international universities, including Strate School of Design in Paris, Duoc UC in Chile and Bauhaus University in Weimar. She is the regional chairwoman of VDID (Association of German Industrial Designers) for north Germany and, in her capacity as a gender expert, has been an evaluator for Femtech in Austria since 2005.

www.designkunst.com

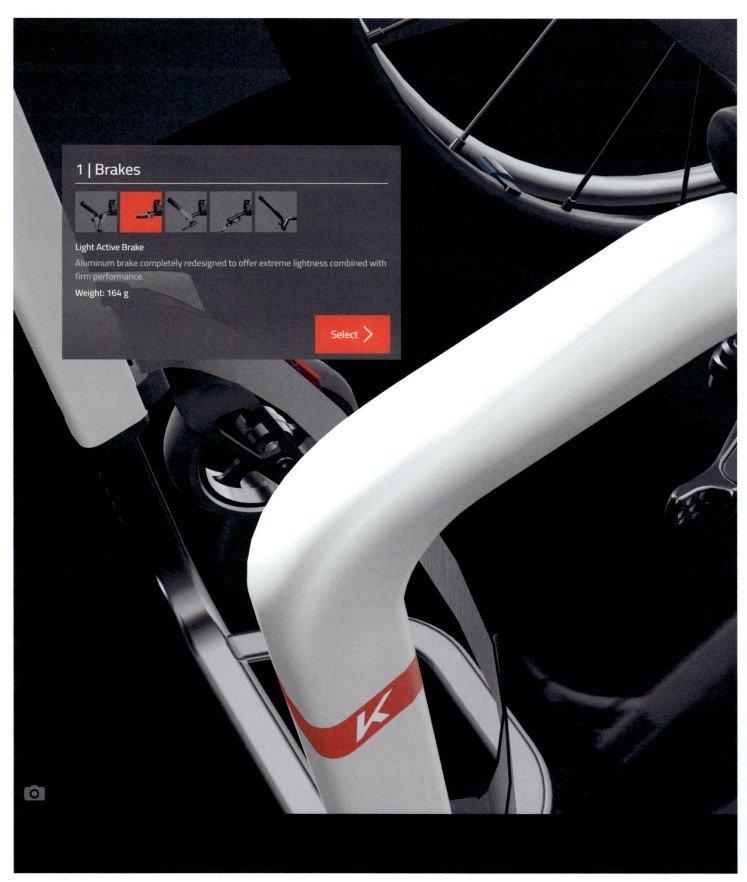

SERVICE DESIGN
SERVICE DESIGN

GOLD:
KÜSCHALL VISUALIZER
Küschall AG
Witterswil
Schweiz / Switzerland

Die Digitalisierung von Produkten und Dienstleistungen schreitet voran – die nutzerzentrierte Gestaltung von Interfaces und Bedienlogiken sorgt dafür, dass die Services in ihrer Tiefe und Funktionalität zu intuitiven Tools werden, die sowohl im virtuellen wie realen Kontext ihren eigentlichen Wert entfalten können.

The digitalisation of products and services is progressing – the user-centric design of interfaces and operating logics makes the depth and functionality of services accessible by turning them into intuitive tools that can demonstrate their true value in both a real and virtual context.

13

GOLD

KÜSCHALL VISUALIZER

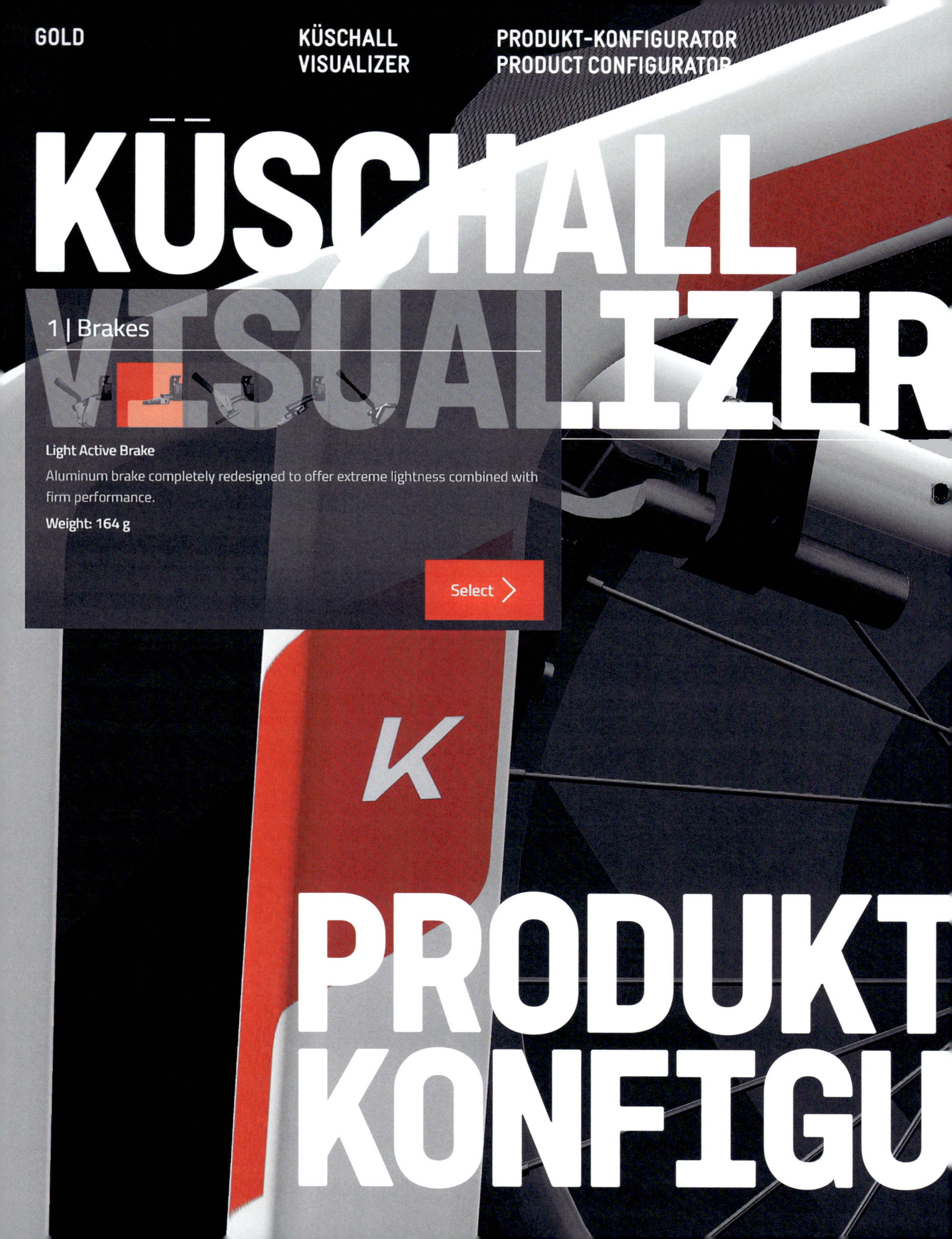

PRODUKT-KONFIGURATOR
PRODUCT CONFIGURATOR

KÜSCHALL VISUALIZER

1 | Brakes

Light Active Brake

Aluminum brake completely redesigned to offer extreme lightness combined with firm performance.

Weight: 164 g

Select >

PRODUKT KONFIGU

1 | Rear wheel diameter

2 | Rear wheel type

Spinergy LXK

Black hub, rim and 18 patented PBO spokes delivering 3-times the strength of stainless steel at just half the weight and a faster responding wheel.

Weight: 1200 g

3 | Rear wheel tyre

Schwalbe One

Puncture resistant with improved compound and quality workmanship. Great puncture protection from the V-Guard, made from a special light fabric.

Weight: 500 g

4 | Handrim

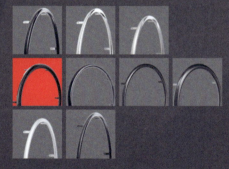

Carbolife GEKKO

Mounted at 3 cm distance. Designed for users with complete hand function and either complete or limited hand strength. The robust silicone strip increases the grip and the anodized low-friction surface at the sides prevents heat generation.

Weight: 1380 g

5 | Rear wheel camber

6 | Rear wheel fixation

GOLD

KÜSCHALL VISUALIZER
PRODUKT-KONFIGURATOR / PRODUCT CONFIGURATOR

JURY STATEMENT

Das browserbasierte Online-Tool ist sehr klar und für alle verständlich aufgebaut. Es reduziert die Komplexität der Rollstuhl-Konfiguration, also die Anpassung auf ganz individuelle Notwendigkeiten und Vorlieben. Sehr nutzer*innenfreundlich ist die dreidimensionale, drehbare Darstellung der vielen Optionen in Echtzeit. Der Visualizer macht vor, wie man hoch individualisierbare Produkte sinnvoll darstellt und ein positives Nutzererlebnis erzeugt.

The way the browser-based online tool is structured is extremely clear and easy to understand. It reduces the complexity of configuring the wheelchair to suit customers' highly individual wants and needs. The three-dimensional, rotatable visualisation of the many different options in real time is extremely user-friendly. The visualiser is a prime example of how to depict highly customisable products in a meaningful way and ensure a positive user experience.

HERSTELLER / MANUFACTURER
Küschall AG
Witterswil
Schweiz / Switzerland

DESIGN
UP Designstudio GmbH & Co. KG
Stuttgart

VERTRIEB / DISTRIBUTOR
Küschall AG
Witterswil
Schweiz / Switzerland

Gerade stark individualisierbare Produkte wie zum Beispiel Rollstühle lassen sich in ihrer Optionsbreite und Kombinierbarkeit mit traditionellen Mitteln kaum darstellen. Der interaktive Konfigurator hingegen zeigt in einem digitalen Präsentationsraum die Gesamtheit aller Möglichkeiten, zugleich aber auch detaillierte Informationen zu den gewählten Komponenten. Nutzer*innen werden intuitiv durch das Portfolio geführt, die Installation spezieller Software ist nicht nötig, ein Standardbrowser reicht für die Darstellung aus. Dennoch werden die individualisierten Rollstühle verzögerungsfrei als 3D-Modelle dargestellt, mitsamt Schatten, Reflexen und Strukturen. Am Ende steht ein Datenblatt des Rollstuhls, das als Bestellbasis dient. Gedacht ist der Konfigurator für die Verkaufsberatung beim Händler oder für die Vorab-Kundeninformation.

Because they permit such a wide range of options and combinations, highly customisable products – like wheelchairs, for instance – are particularly challenging to visualise with traditional means. This interactive configurator is different: it uses a digital showroom to present the entire range of possibilities, while simultaneously providing detailed information about the components selected. Users are guided through the portfolio intuitively without having to install any special software – a standard browser is all that's required. Even so, the customised wheelchairs are instantly depicted as 3D models complete with shadows, reflections and textures. The datasheet generated at the end of the configuration process serves as the basis for ordering the wheelchair. The configurator is intended as a tool for dealers' sales advisors or as a way for customers to inform themselves beforehand.

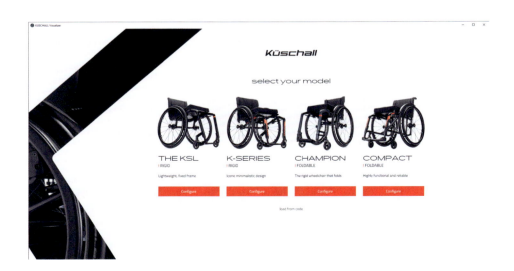

STEFAN LIPPERT   **GESCHÄFTSFÜHRER, UP DESIGNSTUDIO GMBH & CO. KG**

»Der Visualizer lässt sich für alle möglichen Produktarten nutzen, sogar für die Konfiguration komplexer Produktionsanlagen.«

»The visualizer can be used for all sorts of products, even for configuring complex production facilities.«

STEFAN LIPPERT   **MANAGING DIRECTOR, UP DESIGNSTUDIO GMBH & CO. KG**

→ **Online-Konfiguratoren sind nicht unbedingt neu – was ist besonders am Küschall Visualizer?**
Meistens arbeiten Konfiguratoren auf Fotobasis, also mit festen Abbildungen, die sich in bestimmten Grenzen variieren lassen. Der von uns entwickelte Konfigurator hingegen nutzt ein 3D-Datenmodell des Produkts, das in Echtzeit immer wieder neu gerendert wird. Damit lässt sich der Rollstuhl frei bewegen und aus beliebigen Perspektiven betrachten. Man kann seine Funktionsfeatures testen und ihn mit individuellen Zusatzteilen ergänzen.

Für welches Szenario ist der Visualizer gedacht?
Der hier prämierte Visualizer verbessert das Zusammenstellen des eigenen Rollstuhls. Denn der ist ein komplexes Produkt aus vielen verschiedenen Teilprodukten, die in unterschiedlichsten Kombinationen verfügbar sind. Je besser ein Rollstuhl auch in Details den individuellen Anforderungen entspricht, desto größer ist sein Nutzwert. Der Visualizer ist also gleichermaßen ein Tool für das Marketing wie für die Nutzer*innen, er erlaubt, sich eingehend mit dem maßgefertigten Produkt zu beschäftigen.

Lässt sich das Prinzip auch auf andere Anwendungen oder Produkte übertragen?
Ja, natürlich. Gerade bei komplexen Produktsystemen macht sich der Konfigurator bezahlt. Er erleichtert sowohl das Kennenlernen des Produkts, seiner Details und Features als auch das individuelle Zusammenstellen. Es ist aber auch möglich, ihn für Schulungen einzusetzen. Wir können schnell und unabhängig von der Sprache Wissen vermitteln. Im Prinzip ließe sich der Visualizer für alle möglichen Produktarten nutzen, von Medizinprodukten bis hin zu komplexen Produktionsanlagen.

Die Entwicklung des Visualizers dürfte stark technisch geprägt sein – wie kommt das Design ins Spiel?
Das Design ist vor allem durch die User Experience und die Gestaltung des Interfaces präsent. Wir achten darauf, dass die Optionen und auch die Anmutung des Ganzen zur Zielgruppe passen, die Auswahlmöglichkeiten erkennbar sowie nachvollziehbar sind und die Nutzer*innen positiv gestimmt werden.

Das UP Designstudio mit Sitz in Stuttgart wurde in der Vergangenheit bereits mehrfach mit dem Focus Open ausgezeichnet – für Consumer-Produkte ebenso wie für Investitionsgüter. 1994 gegründet, firmierte das Büro lange Jahre als ipdd, seit 2017 ist es als UP Designstudio präsent. Geleitet wird das Studio von Stefan Lippert und Wolf Leonhardt.

www.updesignstudio.de

→ **Online configurators aren't altogether new – what's special about the Küschall Visualizer?**
Configurators are normally based on photos, i.e. on fixed images that can be varied within certain limits. The configurator we developed is different: it uses a 3D data model of the product that is constantly re-rendered in real time. As a result, you can move the wheelchair around and look at it from whatever perspective you like. You can test its optional features and add customised extras.

What kind of scenario is the visualizer intended for?
The visualizer that won the award improves the process of putting your own wheelchair together. After all, a wheelchair is a complex product made up of lots of different components that are available in all sorts of different combinations. The better a wheelchair corresponds to individual requirements, the greater its utility. And that goes for the details too. So the visualizer is a tool for marketing and users alike, because it enables you to explore the custom-made product in depth.

Could the same principle be transferred to other applications or products?
Yes, of course. The configurator is particularly worthwhile when complex product systems are involved. It makes it easier not just to familiarise yourself with the product, its details and features, but to put it together in keeping with your individual needs. And it could be used for training purposes as well, because it conveys knowledge quickly and independently of language. In principle, the visualizer could be used for all sorts of things, from medical products all the way to complex production facilities.

Technology no doubt played a major role in the visualizer's development – where does design come into play with a product like this?
First and foremost, it makes itself felt in the user experience and the design of the interface. We make sure that the options and the look of the whole thing are a good fit with the target group, that the choices are easily recognisable and understandable and that the whole experience leaves users feeling in a good mood.

UP Designstudio is based in Stuttgart and has won several Focus Open awards in the past – for both consumer products and capital goods. Founded in 1994, the firm operated as ipdd for many years before changing its name to UP Designstudio in 2017. The studio is headed by Stefan Lippert and Wolf Leonhardt.

www.updesignstudio.de

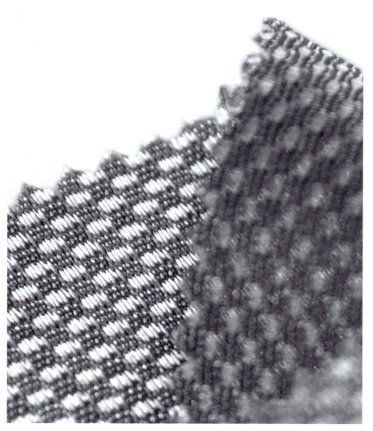

1 → SEITE / PAGE
208–213

2 → SEITE / PAGE
214, 216

3 → SEITE / PAGE
215, 217

MATERIALS + SURFACES

1	**GOLD:** **WIRKUNGSVOLL** Rökona Textilwerke GmbH & Co KG Tübingen
2	**SILVER:** **BIOPROFILE** ETS Extrusionstechnik Stange Mücheln
3	**SPECIAL MENTION:** **PRO ARCHITECTURA 3.0** V&B Fliesen GmbH Merzig

Technik beeinflusst schon immer das Design, auch Werkstoffe tun dies mehr denn je. Materialien mit innovativen Eigenschaften eröffnen Nutzungsszenarien, die zu mehr Nachhaltigkeit, geringerem Ressourcenverbrauch oder optimierter Funktionsintegration leiten.

Technology has always influenced design, and materials are having a greater impact than ever before. Materials with innovative properties open up usage scenarios that lead to greater sustainability, reduced resource consumption or the optimised integration of functions.

GOLD WIRKUNGSVOLL KETTWIRKWARE
WARP-KNITTED FABRICS

WIRKUNGSVOLL

KETTWIRKWARE

GOLD — WIRKUNGSVOLL — KETTWIRKWARE / WARP-KNITTED FABRICS

JURY STATEMENT

Eine Materialentwicklung, die in die richtige Richtung weist und zeigt, dass Verbundmaterialien durchaus verzichtbar sind. Hier knüpft die intelligente Veränderung von Prozessen an die Forderung nach zeitgemäßem Design und Kreislaufwirtschaft an. Obwohl für die Autobranche konzipiert, sollten die Textilien ihren Weg auch in andere Bereiche finden.

A materials development that points in the right direction and shows that composite materials are by no means the only alternative. In this case the intelligent modification of processes is tied to the demand for contemporary design and circular practices. Although initially conceived for the automotive industry, the textiles are also intended to find their way into other areas.

HERSTELLER / MANUFACTURER
Rökona Textilwerk GmbH & Co KG
Tübingen

DESIGN
Inhouse

VERTRIEB / DISTRIBUTOR
Rökona Textilwerk GmbH & Co KG
Tübingen

Nur sortenreine Materialien sind wirtschaftlich recycelbar, das ist hinreichend bekannt. Doch Mono-Materialien stellen Entwickler*innen vor große Herausforderungen, spätestens dann, wenn es um die Kombination verschiedener Eigenschaften geht. Dass es auch anders geht, zeigen die beiden im Wirkverfahren produzierten Textilien für das Interieur von Fahrzeugen, speziell für die Beschattung von Panoramadächern.

Der Glanzgrad der Textilien hängt von der Art ab, wie die einzelnen Fäden gelegt wurden. Je nach Lichteinfall reflektieren die Oberflächen unterschiedlich – bei starkem Licht wirkt die Fläche glänzend, bei wenig Licht ausgesprochen matt. Die metallische Optik entsteht ohne zusätzliche Bedampfung, das Material bleibt komplett metallfrei. Der Wirkprozess lässt sich variieren und bringt verschiedene, metallische Farben hervor.

While it's no secret that only mono-materials can be recycled efficiently, they present developers with major challenges – especially when it comes to combining different characteristics. But there's another way – as demonstrated by these two warp-knitted textiles for vehicle interiors, intended for shading panoramic sunroofs.

The textiles' degree of sheen depends on the way the individual threads were laid. The surfaces reflect differently depending on how the light falls – in strong light the fabrics look shiny, in weak light they appear extremely matt. The metallic effect is produced without the need for an additional coating, ensuring that the material remains completely metal-free. The warp-knitting process can be varied to produce different metallic colours.

KATHARINA SCHÄFER DESIGNERIN,
RÖKONA TEXTILWERK GMBH & CO. KG

»Wir sehen unsere Verantwortung und unseren Einfluss auf den Kreislauf darin, die von uns hergestellten Materialien recyclingfähig zu machen.«

»We believe our responsibility and our influence on circularity lies in making the materials we produce recyclable.«

KATHARINA SCHÄFER
DESIGNER, RÖKONA TEXTILWERK GMBH & CO. KG

→ Sie haben ein Mono-Material mit der optischen Wirkung eines Verbundmaterials entwickelt – welche Herausforderungen gab es da zu meistern?

Ein Verbundmaterial hat den Vorteil, dass es aus zwei völlig unterschiedlich produzierten und gestalteten Seiten bestehen kann, die anschließend zusammengeführt werden. Der große Nachteil liegt allerdings darin, dass bei diesen Materialien ein wirtschaftliches Recycling so gut wie ausgeschlossen ist. Deshalb bestand die Herausforderung darin, ein Gewirke mit zwei Seiten und entsprechend unterschiedlichen Eigenschaften zu entwickeln – mit einem einzigen Prozessschritt, ohne Verklebung.

Mit der Kollektion Wirkungsvoll ist es uns gelungen, dieselben Anforderungen, die an ein Verbundmaterial gestellt werden, mit einem Mono-Aufbau zu erfüllen.

Wie lässt sich die Metallic-Optik ohne entsprechende Bedampfung erreichen?

Die hochwertigen Metalloptiken sind natürlich ein wichtiger Faktor im Gesamtpaket, das aus zeitgemäßem Design, modernster Technologie und Nachhaltigkeit besteht. Für unser Textil sind sowohl die textilen Strukturen als auch die eingesetzten Garne so gewählt, dass sie je nach Lichteinfall auf die Fasern unterschiedliche Reflexionen hervorrufen. Das erzeugt die metallisch anmutende Oberflächenwirkung und sorgt für unterschiedliche Farbwirkungen.

Die Gewirke sind zunächst für den Einsatz im Auto-Interieur gedacht – das Potenzial ist aber größer, oder?

Es ist tatsächlich so, dass beispielsweise automobile Innenraumkonzepte und Trends im Wohn- und Möbeldesign aufeinander folgen und eng beieinanderliegen. Insofern können besondere Ergebnisse, wie das hier entwickelte Textil, in Zukunft auch für die Heimtextilsparte und weitere Bereiche interessant sein.

Die Recyclingfähigkeit ist das eine, sagt aber noch wenig über die tatsächliche Wiederverwendung von Materialien aus. Wie halten Sie das Material im Loop?

Wir entwickeln und fertigen die sogenannte Vorstufe eines Halbzeugs, in diesem Fall beispielsweise das Beschattungstextil für das Panoramadach eines Fahrzeugs. Somit sehen wir unsere Verantwortung und unseren Einfluss auf den Kreislauf darin, die von uns hergestellten Materialien recyclingfähig zu machen. Sortenreinheit spielt dabei eine Rolle, die wir mit unserem Textil erfüllen.

> Die Rökona Textilwerk GmbH & Co. KG, 1963 als Ausgründung aus der Gerhard Rösch GmbH hervorgegangen, hat ihren Sitz in Tübingen. Das inhabergeführte Unternehmen entwickelt und produziert technische Textilien für zahlreiche Produkte aus den Bereichen Mobility und Industrie. Dabei liegt der Fokus verstärkt auf dem Einsatz recyclingfähiger Materialien in textilen Flächen.
>
> www.roekona.de

→ You've developed a monomaterial that looks just like a composite – what challenges had to be overcome to achieve that?

A composite has the advantage that it can consist of two sides that are produced and designed in totally different ways and subsequently brought together. However, the major disadvantage is that it's virtually impossible to recycle these materials economically. That's why the challenge was to develop a knitted fabric with two sides and correspondingly different characteristics – with a single process step and no bonding.

With the Wirkungsvoll collection, we've succeeded in satisfying the same requirements a composite material has to meet with a mono-material.

How do you achieve the metallic effect without using evaporation to deposit it?

The premium metallic effects are obviously an important factor in the overall package, which is a combination of contemporary design, state-of-the-art technology and sustainability. In the case of our fabric, both the textile structures and the yarns used are selected to create different reflections depending on how the light hits the fibres. That's what gives the surface its metallic look and creates different colour effects.

To begin with, the fabrics are intended for use in car interiors – but the potential is bigger, right?

As a matter of fact, concepts for car interiors and trends in furniture and interior design follow one another and are closely related. So in that respect, unusual results like the textile we've developed could well be of interest to the home textiles sector and other areas later on.

Recyclability is one thing, but right now it doesn't tell you much about whether materials are actually reused or not. How do you keep the material in the loop?

We develop and produce the pre-stage of a semi-finished product, in this case the sunscreen fabric for the panoramic roof of a vehicle. So we believe our responsibility and our influence on circularity lies in making the materials we produce recyclable. Mono-materials play a role in that, and that's the benefit our textile delivers.

> Rökona Textilwerk GmbH & Co. KG, which was founded in 1963 as a spin-off of Gerhard Rösch GmbH, is based in Tübingen. The owner-managed company develops and produces technical textiles for numerous products in the fields of mobility and industry with an increasing focus on using recyclable materials in textile surfaces.
>
> www.roekona.de

SILVER   **BIOPROFILE**   **BIOBASIERTE PROFILE**
BIO-BASED PROFILES

➜ **SEITE / PAGE**
216

SPECIAL MENTION | PRO ARCHITECTURA 3.0 | FLIESENKOLLEKTION / TILE COLLECTION

→ SEITE / PAGE 217

SILVER

BIOPROFILE

BIOBASIERTE PROFILE
BIO-BASED PROFILES

> **JURY STATEMENT**
>
> Soll das Bauen nachhaltiger werden, spielen die Materialien eine ganz zentrale Rolle. Biobasierte Kunststoffe aus nachwachsenden Rohstoffen sind höchst interessant, auch weil sie mit herkömmlichen Methoden verarbeitbar sind.
>
> Materials have a key role to play if construction is to become more sustainable. Bio-based plastics made from renewable raw materials are extremely interesting in this context, partly also because they can be processed using conventional methods.

HERSTELLER / MANUFACTURER
ETS Extrusionstechnik Stange
Mücheln

DESIGN
BioMat am ITKE
Stuttgart

Im Rahmen eines Forschungsprojektes entwickelte das Institut für Tragkonstruktion und Konstruktives Entwerfen ITKE der Universität Stuttgart Fassaden- und Fensterprofile, die aus biobasierten Werkstoffen bestehen. Die Profile werden im Extrusions- und Coextrusionsverfahren produziert und enthalten einen hohen Anteil an Strohfasern aus landwirtschaftlichen Resten. Auf diese Weise lassen sich erdölbasierte Kunststoffe ersetzen und die Nachhaltigkeit des Bauens verbessern. Die Biokompositmaterialien weisen sowohl gleichwertige mechanische Eigenschaften auf wie ihre konventionellen Pendants als auch vergleichbare Verarbeitungsbedingungen. Auch lassen sich komplexe Querschnitte extrudieren, wie sie für Fensterprofile notwendig sind.

As part of a research project, the Institute of Building Structures and Structural Design (ITKE) at the University of Stuttgart developed profiles made of bio-based materials for use in facades and windows. The profiles are produced by means of extrusion and co-extrusion processes and contain a high percentage of straw fibres obtained from agricultural waste. As a replacement for profiles made of petroleum-based plastics, they could therefore result in more sustainable construction. Besides having equally good mechanical properties as compared to their conventional counterparts, the processing conditions for the biocomposites are also comparable. What's more, they can be extruded with the kind of complex cross-sections necessary for window profiles.

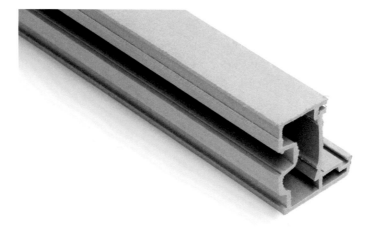

PRO ARCHITECTURA 3.0 — FLIESENKOLLEKTION / TILE COLLECTION

JURY STATEMENT

Die Kollektion begeistert mit ihrer sehr aktuellen und ästhetischen Farbzusammenstellung, die Systematik unterstützt die freie Kombination der Muster und damit die Komposition individueller Farbwelten.

As well as offering an inspiring assortment of very contemporary and aesthetic colours, the system the collection is based on permits a great deal of freedom in terms of putting patterns and therefore individual colour palettes together.

HERSTELLER / MANUFACTURER
V&B Fliesen GmbH
Merzig

DESIGN
Inhouse, mit/with
Prof. Dr. Axel Buether
Wuppertal

VERTRIEB / DISTRIBUTOR
V&B Fliesen GmbH
Merzig

Fliesen gestalten Räume – umso mehr, wenn sie aus hochwertigen Materialien gefertigt sind und ihnen ein individuelles Farbkonzept zu Grunde liegt. Die Fliesenkollektion ist für den Einsatz in architektonischen Räumen mit unterschiedlichen Funktionsbereichen gedacht, vom Kindergarten über das Schwimmbad bis hin zu gastronomischen Bereichen. Verfügbar sind glasierte Steingutfliesen für die Wand, glasiertes Steinzeug und unglasiertes Feinsteinzeug für Wand und Boden in unterschiedlichen Farben. Bei der Entwicklung des Farbsystems waren nicht nur ästhetische Gesichtspunkte ausschlaggebend, sondern auch die Berücksichtigung der Farbwirkung im Raum über den dekorativen Charakter hinaus.

Tiles make rooms – all the more so when they're made of top-quality materials and based on an individual colour concept. This tile collection is intended for use in architectonic spaces with all sorts of different functions, from preschools to swimming pools and restaurants. It includes glazed non-vitreous tiles for the wall as well as glazed vitreous and unglazed porcelain stoneware for the wall and floor, all available in different colours. Besides aesthetic aspects, the impact the colours have on the space beyond their purely decorative effect was a key consideration in the development of the colour system.

MIA SEEGER PREIS 2021

MIA SEEGER PREIS 2021

Jährlicher Wettbewerb der Mia Seeger Stiftung
für junge Designerinnen und Designer
mit Unterstützung der Hans Schwörer Stiftung und
des Rat für Formgebung

The Mia Seeger Foundation's annual
competition for young designers,
sponsored by the Hans Schwörer Foundation
and the German Design Council

MIA SEEGER PREIS 2021 — GEWONNEN HABEN …
MIA SEEGER PRIZE 2021 — THE WINNERS ARE …

1 → SEITE / PAGE 224
2 → SEITE / PAGE 225
3 → SEITE / PAGE 226
4 → SEITE / PAGE 227

5 → SEITE / PAGE 228
6 → SEITE / PAGE 228
7 → SEITE / PAGE 229
8 → SEITE / PAGE 230

9 → SEITE / PAGE 230
10 → SEITE / PAGE 231
11 → SEITE / PAGE 232
12 → SEITE / PAGE 232

13 → SEITE / PAGE 233
14 → SEITE / PAGE 234
15 → SEITE / PAGE 234
16 → SEITE / PAGE 235

MIA SEEGER PREIS 2021
MIA SEEGER PRIZE 2021

PARTIKULAR
1 Dennis Nogard

ANA
2 Charlotte Schierning

DIALYSE UNTERWEGS /
DIALYSIS ON THE GO
3 Paola Andrea Aldana Vidal

ANERKENNUNG
HIGHLY COMMENDED

INTIMUS
4 Ruben Geörge

ROLLAID
5 Mia Pahl
und / and
6 Julian Kufner

PEBBLE
7 Jana Koßenjans

RECOVER
8 Konstantin Wolf
und / and
9 Min Zhang

FLEXION
10 David Rieche

LEIPS
11 Moritz Robert Hartstang
und / and
12 Tara Monheim

VERTICAL GAMES
13 Leo Stolte

DER GLÄSERNE STAAT /
THE TRANSPARENT STATE
14 Julia Sophie Thum
und / and
15 Winona Biber

WATEREPUBLIC
16 Jadwiga Slezak

MIA SEEGER PREIS 2021
MIA SEEGER PRIZE 2021

10.000 EURO FÜR JUNGE DESIGNERINNEN UND DESIGNER
€10,000 FOR YOUNG DESIGNERS

JURY

PROF. ANNE BERGNER
Designerin,
Akademie der Bildenden Künste
Stuttgart / Designer,
Stuttgart Academy of Art and Design

MATTHIS HAMANN
Designer,
Managing Partner, Fluid GmbH,
München / Designer, managing
partner, Fluid GmbH, Munich

STEFAN LIPPERT
Designer,
UP Designstudio, Stuttgart,
Mia Seeger Preisträger
1993 und Stipendiat 1993/94 /
Designer, UP Designstudio,
Stuttgart, Mia Seeger
prize winner 1993 and
scholarship winner 1993/94

ARMIN SCHARF
Freier Journalist,
Tübingen / Freelance journalist,
Tübingen

OLIVER STOTZ
Industriedesigner,
stotz-design.com, Wuppertal,
Mia Seeger Preisträger 1992 / Industrial
designer, stotz-design.com,
Wuppertal, Mia Seeger prize winner

Alles im alten Gleis wieder? – Nein. In der zweiten Welle von Corona schrieb die Mia Seeger Stiftung erneut ihren Preis aus. Weiterhin alles digital. Einreichungen übers Internet, Anlegen von Dateien, Jurieren unterm Bildschirm. Allen, die sich wieder ins Zeug gelegt haben (siehe Jury und Impressum), sei von Herzen gedankt. Der Mühe Lohn waren 91 Anmeldungen aus 27 Hochschulen. An die eingereichten Arbeiten hatte die Jury neben den üblichen Qualitätsmaßstäben den des sozialen Nutzens anzulegen. Resultat: drei Preise und neun Anerkennungen.

Everything back to normal? No. The Mia Seeger Foundation's call for entries for this year's competition came in the second wave of the corona pandemic. Everything still digital. Submissions via the internet, countless files created, some jurors present only on screen. So once again, a big thank you to everyone who made it happen (see Jury and Publishing Details). All the effort paid off: 91 entries were received from 27 colleges and universities. In addition to the usual quality criteria, the jury also assessed the works submitted on the basis of their benefit to society. The result: three prizes and nine Highly Commended distinctions.

Die Jury am 15. Juli 2021. Von links:
Armin Scharf, Anne Bergner,
Matthis Hamann, Oliver Stotz,
Stefan Lippert.

The jury on 15 July 2021. From left:
Armin Scharf, Anne Bergner,
Matthis Hamann, Oliver Stotz,
Stefan Lippert.

© Florin Betz

MIA SEEGER PREIS 2021
MIA SEEGER PRIZE 2021

PARTIKULAR – UNKRAUTREGULIERUNG PER ROBOTER
PARTIKULAR – WEED CONTROL BY ROBOT

ENTWERFER/DEVELOPER
Dennis Nogard
dennis@nogard.de

STUDIUM/DEGREE COURSE
Produktdesign, M.A.
Weißensee Kunsthochschule Berlin

BETREUUNG/SUPERVISORS
Prof. Nils Krüger
Prof. Dr. Jörg Petruschat

Ein brückenartiges Konstrukt schiebt sich auf Raupenfahrwerken übers Feld, in der Mitte ein Tank für Splitt aus Biomaterial (z.B. Maiskolben) mit Schlauchverbindungen zu sechs Sprühköpfen. Mittels Bilderkennung dirigiert die Steuerung die Düsen genau dahin, wo Unkraut wächst. Ein kurzer, kräftiger Strahl splitthaltiger Druckluft und die zerschredderten Pflanzen bleiben samt Splitt als Düngemittel auf dem Feld zurück.

A bridge-like construction moves across the field on a chassis equipped with caterpillar tracks; in the middle, a tank for chippings made of biomaterial (e.g. corncobs), fitted with hoses that connect it to six spray heads. Using image recognition, the control system targets the jets at precisely the places where weeds are growing. A short, powerful burst of chipping-laden compressed air, and the shredded plants are left behind on the field along with the chippings as fertiliser.

JURY STATEMENT

Starkes Industriedesign für einen Agrarroboter. Eine intelligente Sprühmechanik macht Herbizide entbehrlich. Selektive Unkrautregulierung löst flächendeckende Unkrautvernichtung ab. Tragwerk und die breiten Raupen sind auf möglichst geringe Bodenbelastung berechnet. Dank Klappmechanik lässt sich auch der Transport von und zum Feld gut bewerkstelligen.

Strong industrial design for an agricultural robot. An intelligent spraying mechanism dispenses with the need for herbicides. Selective weed control supersedes blanket spraying with weed killer. The supporting structure and wide caterpillar tracks are calculated to impact the soil as little as possible and the folding mechanism makes light work of transporting the robot to and from the field.

MIA SEEGER PREIS 2021
MIA SEEGER PRIZE 2021

ANA – EINE NISTHILFE FÜR HUMMELN
ANA – A NESTING AID FOR BUMBLEBEES

ENTWERFERIN / DEVELOPER
Charlotte Schierning
charlotte.schierning@gmx.de

STUDIUM / DEGREE COURSE
Industriedesign, M.A.
Muthesius Kunsthochschule Kiel

BETREUUNG / SUPERVISORS
Prof. Detlef Rhein
Prof. Dr. Norbert M. Schmitz

Eine Höhle aus klimaregulierender Keramik mit einem Einsatz aus Pappe. Beides ist so bemessen, dass eine Hummel darin ihr Nest bauen kann. Ein Instrument der Analyse wird die Nisthilfe durch die Messtechnik am Eingang. Kameras und Sensoren bestimmen Hummelart, Flugfrequenz, Beifang an Pollen, Luftfeuchtigkeit und Temperatur im Inneren. Datenerhebung und -auswertung sind gedacht für umwelt- und agrarpolitische Programme auf nationaler und europäischer Ebene.

A cave of climate-regulating ceramic with a cardboard insert, both gauged so that a bumblebee can build its nest inside. The measuring technology at the entrance turns the nesting aid into an analysis tool. Cameras and sensors determine the species of bumblebee, flight frequency and pollen bycatch, as well as the humidity and temperature inside. The data collection and analysis are intended for environmental and agricultural policy programmes at national and European level.

JURY STATEMENT

Natürlich geht es darum, dem Insektensterben gegenzusteuern. Auch die Leute aus der Landwirtschaft werden als zentrale Akteure in die Pflicht genommen: die Nisthilfen aufstellen und pflegen, dort die Daten abrufen und an eine Zentrale übermitteln. Arbeiten, die ihnen angesichts der praktisch geteilten und sehr sympathischen Gehäuseform auch genehm gemacht werden.

It goes without saying that the design is all about combating insect extinction. It seeks to involve those in the agricultural sector as key players, charged with setting up and taking care of the nesting aids, retrieving the data and passing it on to a central agency. The practically divided and very appealing form of the housing promise to make such tasks anything but arduous.

MIA SEEGER PREIS 2021
MIA SEEGER PRIZE 2021

DIALYSE UNTERWEGS
DIALYSIS ON THE GO

ENTWERFERIN / DEVELOPER
Paola Andrea Aldana Vidal
paoaldana94@hotmail.com

STUDIUM / DEGREE COURSE
Produktdesign, B.A.
Weißensee Kunsthochschule Berlin

BETREUUNG / SUPERVISORS
Prof. Nils Krüger
Prof. Lucy Norris

Was wie eine ausgepolsterte Weste aussieht, ist als voll funktionsfähiges Dialysegerät konzipiert, für das es normalerweise ein halbes Krankenzimmer braucht. Etliche Komponenten sind eigens so umgestaltet, dass sie sich in das dicht und flach gepackte Ensemble von Behältern, Schläuchen, Ventilen, Pumpen, Aggregaten und Batterien einfügen.

What looks like a padded waistcoat is in fact a concept for a fully functional dialysis machine – something that would normally take up half a hospital room. A number of components have been specially redesigned to fit into the densely and flatly packed ensemble of containers, tubes, valves, pumps, controls and batteries.

JURY STATEMENT

Eine stationäre Apparatur ist Stück für Stück auf minimalen Platzbedarf und flache Bauweise umgearbeitet – immer mit dem Gedanken daran, wie alles in einem Kleidungsstück tragbar unterzubringen sei. An der Krankheit ändert das nichts, gewinnt ihr aber Unabhängigkeit ab. Wer dennoch Scheu hat, kann die Weste unter Jacke oder Pullover tragen.

A stationary apparatus has been reworked piece by piece to minimise the space required and turn it into a »flatpack« – while never losing sight of the idea that the end result has to fit into a piece of clothing and be wearable. Although that doesn't do anything to change the illness, it does promise independence from it. And those who feel self-conscious can always put the waistcoat on under a jacket or sweater.

ANERKENNUNG
HIGHLY COMMENDED

INTIMUS – VERHÜTUNG FÜR DEN MANN
INTIMUS – MALE CONTRACEPTION

ENTWERFER/DEVELOPER
Ruben Geörge
rubengeoerge@yahoo.de

STUDIUM/DEGREE COURSE
Strategische Gestaltung, M.A.
Hochschule für Gestaltung Schwäbisch Gmünd

BETREUUNG/SUPERVISORS
Prof. Gabriele Niki Reichert
Prof. Dr. habil. Georg Kneer

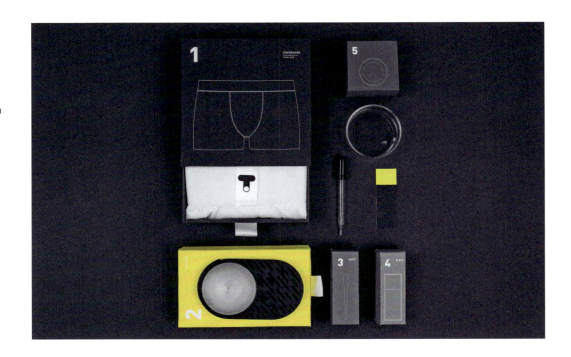

Verhüterli nein danke. Aber etwas anderes bleibt dem Mann zu tun: Er kann eine Unterhose tragen – mit Heizelement, das die Hoden erwärmt, bis die Spermien steril sind. Ein kleines Prüfgerät verschafft ihm in diesem Punkt Sicherheit. Alles, was er für die thermische Familienplanung braucht, ist in einem Paket zusammengestellt. Eine App hilft ihm bei der Anwendung.

Condoms? No thanks! But there's something else a man can do: he can wear underpants – with a heating element that warms the testicles until the sperm are sterile. A little testing device provides certainty. Everything he needs for his thermal family planning has been put together in a kit, with an accompanying app that explains how to use it.

JURY STATEMENT

Ein ernsthaftes Produkt oder eher ein Ablenkungsmanöver in der Gleichberechtigungsdebatte? Der Autor lässt keinen Zweifel. Nach einer materialreichen historisch-soziologischen Recherche zu Sexualität und Verhütung setzt er das aus der Forschung bekannte thermische Verfahren in ein Produkt um und malt sich aus, wie für dessen Akzeptanz zu werben wäre.

A serious product or just a distraction in the equality debate? The author leaves no doubt. After studying extensive historical-sociological materials on sexuality and contraception, he has translated the thermal procedure familiar from research into a product and envisions how to promote acceptance of it.

**ANERKENNUNG
HIGHLY COMMENDED**

**ROLLAID – ROLLATOR IM ALLTAG
ROLLAID – A WHEELED WALKER AS EVERYDAY HELPER**

ENTWERFER*IN / DEVELOPERS
Mia Pahl
mia.pahl@freenet.de
und / and
Julian Kufner
julian-kufner@web.de

STUDIUM / DEGREE COURSE
Produktgestaltung
Hochschule für Gestaltung Schwäbisch Gmünd

BETREUUNG / SUPERVISOR
Dozent Andreas Hess

Wer sich beim Gehen schwertut, kommt im Allgemeinen mit einem handelsüblichen Rollator ganz gut zurecht. Nur beim Aufstehen hilft keiner. Dieser hier schon. Ein zweites Paar Griffe löst das Problem. Dabei bietet sich die Gelegenheit, mit dem Materialmix Metall/Holz dem Rollator einen wohnlicheren Anstrich zu geben.

In general, people who have trouble walking manage perfectly well with a standard rollator. But it's no help when it comes to getting on their feet in the first place. This walker is different: it solves the problem with a second pair of handles. At the same time, the mix of metal and wood is a welcome opportunity to give the rollator a warmer, friendlier look.

JURY STATEMENT

Indem sie eine vorhandene stationäre Aufstehhilfe mit ihren Zusatzgriffen ausstatteten, konnten die beiden Studierenden im Test mit einer Seniorin zeigen, dass ihr Ansatz richtig ist. Mehr Alltagstauglichkeit, die auch die Betreuer um ebenso viel entlastet, als sie die Nutzer selbständiger macht.

By equipping an existing stationary sit-to-stand aid with their extra handles, the two students were able to demonstrate that their approach is right in a test with a senior. The result is more everyday practicality that not only gives users greater independence but makes life easier for their carers as well.

ANERKENNUNG
HIGHLY COMMENDED

PEBBLE – BEWEGT SENIOREN
PEBBLE – SMART MOVES FOR SENIORS

ENTWERFERIN/DEVELOPER
Jana Koßenjans
Jana.Kossenjans@web.de

STUDIUM/DEGREE COURSE
Industrial Design, B.A.
Hochschule Osnabrück

BETREUUNG/SUPERVISORS
Prof. Bastian Beate
Prof. Marian Dziubiel

Fit im Alter. Die richtigen Bewegungsübungen vorzuschreiben und die genaue Ausführung mit Sensoren in einem handgeführten Ball zu kontrollieren, das ist mit einer App auf dem Handy gut zu machen. Die Motivation ist das Problem. Ein Trainingspartner, gegen den anzutreten wäre, ist die Lösung.

When it comes to keep fit for the elderly, prescribing the right exercises and using the sensors in a handheld ball to check that they're being performed correctly is straightforward enough with the right smartphone app. It's motivation that's the problem. The solution: a training partner to compete against.

JURY STATEMENT

Freundliche, ausreichend auffällige Farbe, eingängige Figuren und leichte Sprache sind wohl altersgerecht – state of the art. Der entscheidende Kunstgriff ist aber, die der Ertüchtigung bedürftigen Personen aus der Reserve zu locken: Der Wettbewerb mit einem realen oder fiktiven Partner stachelt ihren Ehrgeiz an.

A cheerful, sufficiently eye-catching colour, comprehensible characters and simple language are doubtless age-appropriate – state of the art. But the absolutely crucial trick is to bring those in need of exercise out of their shell: competing with a real or fictional partner will spur them on.

ANERKENNUNG
HIGHLY COMMENDED

RECOVER – BEWEGUNGSAKTIVE SCHULTERORTHESE
RECOVER – MOVEMENT-ACTIVATING SHOULDER ORTHOSIS

ENTWERFER*IN / DEVELOPERS
Konstantin Wolf
wolf-konstantin1@web.de
und / and
Min Zhang
minzhang0852@gmail.com

STUDIUM / DEGREE COURSE
Integriertes Produktdesign, B.A.
Hochschule Coburg

BETREUUNG / SUPERVISOR
Prof. Wolfgang Schabbach

Ein Funktionsstrang aus künstlichen CNT-Muskeln mit Drucksensoren umschließt Arm und Schulter. Je nach Bewegungsart erzeugt das textile Material komplexe Bewegungsmuster. Sie unterstützen die Eigenbewegung, ersetzen sie aber nicht. Je weiter die Heilung fortschreitet, umso weniger Unterstützung.

A band of artificial CNT muscles with pressure sensors surrounds the arm and shoulder. In keeping with the type of movement, the textile material generates complex movement patterns that support the user's own movements without replacing them. The more the healing process progresses, the less support is provided.

JURY STATEMENT

Als wollte die Orthese zum kranken Muskel sagen: Hilf dir selbst, so helf ich dir. Auf diesem Prinzip baut ein spezielles Konzept von Rehabilitation auf und wird im vorliegenden Entwurf nach sorgfältiger Recherche mit einer Komposition von smarten Materialien intelligent umgesetzt.

It's as if the orthosis is trying to tell the injured muscle something: »I'll help you to help yourself.« This principle is the basis for a specific rehabilitation concept and, following careful research, has been intelligently implemented with a combination of smart materials.

ANERKENNUNG
HIGHLY COMMENDED

FLEXION – REFLEXE MESSEN
FLEXION – MEASURING REFLEXES

ENTWERFER/DEVELOPER
David Rieche
davidrieche@gmail.com

STUDIUM/DEGREE COURSE
Medical Design, M.A.
Muthesius Kunsthochschule Kiel

BETREUUNG/SUPERVISORS
Prof. Detlef Rhein
Prof. Dr. Norbert M. Schmitz

Raffinierte Sensortechnik ersetzt das bekannte Hämmerchen. Jetzt werden nur noch zwei unterschiedlich ausgeprägte Sonden an verschiedenen Hautstellen aufgesetzt. Mit der geeigneten Datenbank im Hintergrund lassen sich aus dem gemessenen Reflexbild frühzeitig neurologische Erkrankungen diagnostizieren.

Sophisticated sensor technology replaces the familiar little hammer. Now it's just a case of placing two differently shaped probes on the skin in various places. Backed up by a suitable database, the reflex measurements can be used to diagnose neurological disease at an early stage.

JURY STATEMENT

Die filigrane Grundgestalt der Instrumente entspricht ihrer Aufgabe, feinste Ströme zu messen. Für Funktionsbereiche wie Kontakte zur Haut, Greifzone und Drehschalter sind jeweils passende Materialien gewählt und deren Oberflächen zweckentsprechend veredelt. Wenn es nicht im Einsatz ist, liegt das hochwertige Besteck in einer gleichwertigen Ladeschale.

The slender basic shape of the instruments reflects their task of measuring tiny electric currents. Various suitable materials have been used for functional areas like the contacts that touch the patient's skin, the gripping zone and the rotary switch, and their surfaces finished in keeping with their purpose. When not in use, the valuable instruments are placed on an equally high-quality charging tray.

ANERKENNUNG
HIGHLY COMMENDED

LEIPS – INKLUSIONSSPIEL
LEIPS – INCLUSION GAME

ENTWERFER*IN/DEVELOPERS
Moritz Robert Hartstang
moritz.hartstang@web.de
und/and
Tara Monheim
taramonheim@me.com

STUDIUM/DEGREE COURSE
Produktgestaltung
Hochschule für Gestaltung Schwäbisch Gmünd

BETREUUNG/SUPERVISOR
Prof. Gerhard Reichert

Ein Spiel, das Menschen mit und ohne Beeinträchtigung spielen können. Ohne dezidiert ein Lernspiel zu sein, bringt es die Spieler dahin, dass sie sich mit Braille, lateinischen Buchstaben und Gebärden verständigen. Die Spielkarten und ein mechanischer Übersetzer helfen dabei.

A game that can be played by people with and without disabilities. Without being overtly educational, it gets players to communicate by means of Braille, Latin letters and gestures. The playing cards and a mechanical translator provide assistance.

JURY STATEMENT

Das Spiel trainiert die Hilfsbereitschaft und Kommunikation untereinander. So überbrückt es Arten und Grade von Seh- oder Hörschwäche. Die Beteiligten erleben es als Erfolg, wenn die eigene mit der jeweils anderen Perspektive übereinstimmt. Das befördert die Inklusion.

The game trains players to be helpful and communicate with one another. As a result, it bridges different types and degrees of visual and hearing impairments. Those involved experience a feeling of success when their own perspective corresponds to somebody else's. That promotes inclusion.

ANERKENNUNG
HIGHLY COMMENDED

VERTICAL GAMES
VERTICAL GAMES

ENTWERFER/DEVELOPER
Leo Stolte
leo.stolte@uni-weimar.de

STUDIUM/DEGREE COURSE
Produktdesign
Bauhaus-Universität Weimar

BETREUUNG/SUPERVISORS
Prof. Wolfgang Sattler
Dipl.-Des. Timm Burkhardt

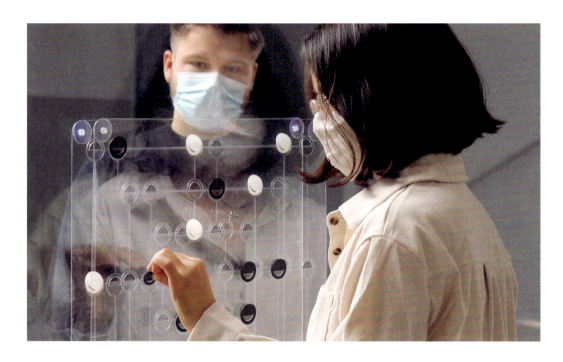

»Nähe auf Distanz« ist das Motto für dieses Spiel. Spielbrett und -figuren sind aus Kunststofffolie. Die Figuren werden in das Brett eingehängt, dieses mit Saugnäpfen an senkrechten Glasflächen aller Art befestigt – überall wo sich Menschen getrennt durch Scheiben begegnen. Das schafft Gelegenheit zu spielerischer Interaktion.

»Closeness at a distance« is the motto for this game. The board and playing pieces are made of plastic film. The pieces are hooked into the board, which can be attached to glass surfaces of any kind with suction cups – wherever people encounter one another with a sheet of glass between them. That creates the opportunity for playful interaction.

JURY STATEMENT

Im Lockdown allgemein und speziell an den omnipräsenten, dem Aerosolschutz dienenden Scheiben entzündete sich die Spielidee. Offensichtlich mildert das Spiel die Isolation und hilft, Trennung zu ertragen. Den Anflug von Poesie spürt, wer als Kind gegen kalte Fensterscheiben gehaucht hat.

The idea for the game was sparked by the lockdown in general, and by the omnipresent panes of glass installed to provide protection from aerosol transmission in particular. The game evidently mitigates the sense of isolation and makes separation more bearable. Its poetry will be appreciated by anyone who breathed onto cold window panes as a child.

ANERKENNUNG
HIGHLY COMMENDED

ENTWERFERINNEN / DEVELOPERS
Julia Sophie Thum
julia-sophie.thum@gmx.de
und / and
Winona Biber
winona.biber@web.de

STUDIUM / DEGREE COURSE
Strategische Gestaltung, M.A.
Hochschule für Gestaltung Schwäbisch Gmünd

BETREUUNG / SUPERVISORS
Prof. Gabriele Niki Reichert
Prof. Dr. habil. Georg Kneer

DER GLÄSERNE STAAT
THE TRANSPARENT STATE

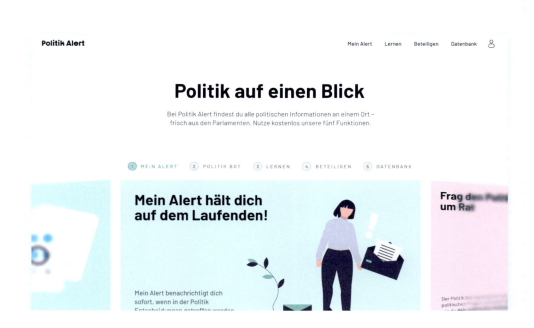

In Rechtspopulismus und Verschwörungstheorien sehen die Autorinnen der Thesis eine Vertrauenskrise und in transparenter Politik ein geeignetes Gegenmittel. Als solches schlagen sie eine Internetplattform vor: »Politik Alert«. Sie informiert aktuell, empfiehlt Formen der Beteiligung, stellt Lehrpläne für Politikwissen auf und bietet Zugang zu geeigneten Datenbanken.

The authors of this thesis see right-wing populism and conspiracy theories as a crisis of confidence and transparent politics as a suitable antidote. And that is precisely what their proposed online platform aims to be: its name translates as »Politics Alert«. It delivers up-to-date information, recommends forms of involvement, outlines programmes for political literacy and provides access to suitable databases.

JURY STATEMENT

Eine enorm umfangreiche Arbeit zu einem brennend aktuellen Thema, zugleich ein unübersehbares Engagement für die parlamentarische Demokratie. Der Ansatz »Vertrauen durch Transparenz« und seine Aufgliederung in fünf Säulen ist plausibel dargelegt und akribisch ausgearbeitet.

A hugely comprehensive piece of work on a highly topical subject, and at the same time a striking declaration of commitment to parliamentary democracy. The approach of creating »confidence through transparency« and its breakdown into five pillars is plausibly presented and meticulously elaborated.

ANERKENNUNG
HIGHLY COMMENDED

WATEREPUBLIC – ÖFFENTLICHE WASSERSTELLE
WATEREPUBLIC – PUBLIC HYDRANT

ENTWERFERIN/DEVELOPER
Jadwiga Slezak
jadjaslezak@gmail.com

STUDIUM/DEGREE COURSE
Industriedesign, M.A.
Muthesius Kunsthochschule Kiel

BETREUUNG/SUPERVISORS
Prof. Detlef Rhein
Prof.in Dr. Annika Frye

Hydranten sind sowieso schon da: für Feuerwehr und Stadtreinigung. Dort eine Zapfsäule für jedermann aufzustellen, an der die Leute trinken, Hände waschen, Gesicht kühlen, Gießwasser für Pflanzen holen, ihre Trinkflasche füllen oder einfach nur herumspritzen können – das würde doch den Platz, die Straße, den Park, den Spielplatz beleben.

Hydrants are already part of the urban scenery anyway. They're used by firefighters and municipal cleaning services. Turning them into a publicly accessible pump where people can drink, wash their hands, cool their faces, fill up their watering cans and drinking bottles or simply splash around would invigorate town squares, streets, parks and playgrounds.

JURY STATEMENT

Der Nutzen für das lokale Klima, für die Aufenthaltsqualität an Plätzen und in Straßen ist unbestritten. Die Gestaltung gliedert die Säule klar in Tränke oben und unten die Anschlüsse für die Feuerwehr und zur privaten Nutzung. Zwar schließt sie an das technische Erscheinungsbild roher Hydranten an, mildert es aber dezent ab.

The benefit for the local climate, for the quality of the time spent in public squares and streets, is incontestable. The design clearly separates the hydrant into a »watering place« at the top and connections for the fire brigade and private usage at the bottom. Although it echoes the technical appearance of basic hydrants, it softens the overall look with subtle modifications.

MIA SEEGER STIFTUNG

THE MIA SEEGER FOUNDATION

IMPRESSUM / PUBLISHING DETAILS

HERAUSGEBER / PUBLISHED BY
Mia Seeger Stiftung

REDAKTION / EDITORS
Marion Ascherl, Schwäbisch Gmünd
Wolfgang Berger, Stuttgart

ÜBERSETZUNG / TRANSLATION
Alison Du Bovis, Jork

GRAFIKDESIGN / GRAPHIC DESIGN
stapelberg & fritz, Stuttgart

AUSSTELLUNGSGESTALTUNG / EXHIBITION DESIGN
Thomas Simianer, Stuttgart

FOTOS / PHOTOS
Preisträger, Ausgezeichnete /
Prizewinners, commended entrants

KOORDINATION MIT »FOCUS OPEN« / COORDINATION WITH FOCUS OPEN
Hildegard Hild

JURYVORBEREITUNG / JUDGING ORGANISED BY
Renate Seeger, Iris Steinmetz,
Marion Ascherl, Team UP Designstudio

DIGITALE TECHNIK, VIDEO-KONFERENZEN / DIGITAL TECHNOLOGY, VIDEO CONFERENCES
Stefan Lippert, UP Designstudio

MIA SEEGER STIFTUNG
c/o Design Center
Baden-Württemberg
im Haus der Wirtschaft
Willi-Bleicher-Straße 19
D-70174 Stuttgart

T +49 711 123 2781
F +49 711 123 2771

E-Mail: design@rps.bwl.de
www.mia-seeger.de
instagram.com/miaseeger

Mia Seeger war die »Grande Dame« des Design. Mit der Weißenhofsiedlung 1927 in Stuttgart begann ihre Laufbahn. Bald war sie an weiteren Ausstellungen des Deutschen Werkbundes beteiligt. Die Bundesrepublik hat sie vielfach als Kommissarin zu Triennalen in Mailand entsandt und zur ersten Leiterin des Rat für Formgebung berufen, den sie zwölf Jahre lang führte. Sie war selbst keine Designerin, sondern Design-Vermittlerin und -Beraterin. 1986 rief sie die nach ihr benannte Stiftung ins Leben, deren Zweck die Bildung junger Gestalterinnen und Gestalter ist. Namhafte Sponsoren aus der Wirtschaft haben sich ihren Zielen angeschlossen.

Mit der Absicht, besonders den Nachwuchs im Design zu fördern und ihn dabei zur Auseinandersetzung mit sozialen Fragen aufzufordern, schreibt die Stiftung jährlich den Mia Seeger Preis unter dem Motto »was mehr als einem nützt« aus. Seit Jahren kann sie die Ergebnisse ihres Designwettbewerbs im Rahmen der Ausstellung »Focus Open – Internationaler Designpreis Baden-Württemberg« präsentieren. Dafür ist sie dem Design Center sehr dankbar, auch für die Vorbereitung und Organisation der Jurierung.

Darüber hinaus erfreut sich die Stiftung schon länger einer vertraglich vereinbarten Kooperation mit dem Rat für Formgebung. Er trägt auch dazu bei, das Wirken der Stiftung, insbesondere die Kontinuität des Mia Seeger Preises finanziell zu sichern. Auch andere Spender haben mit einmaligen Zuwendungen dazu beigetragen, 2016 Alexander Neumeister und im Jahr danach die Hans Schwörer Stiftung. Wer in dieser oder ähnlicher Weise die gemeinnützige Arbeit der Mia Seeger Stiftung unterstützen möchte, wendet sich am besten an die Geschäftsführerin der Stiftung, Marion Ascherl.

Mia Seeger was the »grande dame« of design. Her career began with the Weissenhof Estate in Stuttgart in 1927. She was soon involved with further exhibitions by the Deutscher Werkbund as well. The Federal Republic of Germany frequently sent her to the Triennial exhibitions in Milan as its commissioner and appointed her the first director of the German Design Council, which she headed for twelve years. She herself was not a designer but a design mediator and adviser. She established the foundation that bears her name in 1986 for the purpose of promoting young designers' education. Renowned sponsors from commerce and industry have joined the foundation in the pursuit of its goals.

With the specific aim of promoting young designers and challenging them to tackle social issues, the foundation invites entries for the annual Mia Seeger Prize under the motto »benefiting more than the individual«. For some years now, it has been able to present the results of its design competition within the context of the Focus Open – Baden-Württemberg International Design Award. The foundation is deeply obliged to the Design Center for its assistance, as well as for the preparation and organisation of the judging.

In addition, the foundation has had a cooperation agreement with the German Design Council for some time now. This contract helps ensure the financial security of the foundation's work, and in particular the continuity of the Mia Seeger Prize. Other benefactors have also provided valuable support in the form of one-off donations, including Alexander Neumeister in 2016 and the Hans Schwörer Foundation in the following year. Anybody who would like to support the Mia Seeger Foundation's non-profit work in this or a similar way should please contact the foundation's managing director Marion Ascherl.

Über ihre Arbeit informiert die Stiftung auf ihrer Internetseite: www.mia-seeger.de. Darüber hinaus gibt es News und Posts rund um Design mit sozialem Anspruch auf instagram.com/miaseeger.

Detailed information about the foundation's work is available on its website: www.mia-seeger.de. The foundation also publishes news and posts about design with a social slant at Instagram.com/miaseeger.

APPENDIX
A—Z

ADRESSEN / ADDRESSES

A

AMF – Andreas Maier GmbH & Co. KG
Waiblinger Str. 116
70734 Fellbach
T +49 711/57 660
www.amf.de
S/P 21

B

b+a Vertriebs GmbH
Dammstr. 4
74360 Ilsfeld
T +49 7062/978 910
www.promokick.de
S/P 148

Bene GmbH
Schwarzwiesenstr. 3
A-3340 Waidhofen an der Ybbs
T +43 7442/500
www.bene.com
S/P 83
Christian Horner
S/P 83

Bene GmbH
Adams-Lehmann-Str. 56
80797 München
T +49 89/35 873 710
www.bene.com
S/P 83

bKing Design
Fachschulstr. 18
94227 Zwiesel
T +49 9922/5 004 287
www.bking.de
S/P 107
Bernadett King
S/P 107

Botta Design
Klosterstr. 15a
61462 Königstein/Taunus
T +49 6174/961 188
www.botta-design.de
S/P 106

C

Code2Design
Parkstr. 37
73760 Ostfildern
T +49 711/51 892 844
www.code2design.de
S/P 33

D

Daytona Europe
Monkeyshop
Scheibenstandsweg 5c
30559 Hannover
T +49 177/3 322 014
www.daytona-europe.com
S/P 193

Daytona Corporation
4805 Ichimiya, Mori-machi,
Shuchi-gun
437-0226 Shizuoka
Japan
T +81 538/842 220
www.daytona.co.jp
S/P 193
Nikolaus Tams, Bernd Huth
S/P 193

Defortec GmbH
Breitwasenring 15
72135 Dettenhausen
T +49 7157/7 211 820
www.defortec.de
S/P 31, 179

Designstudio Speziell
Fleckenstein Pohlmann Schwer GbR
Andréstr. 51
63067 Offenbach
T +49 69/80 085 430
www.speziell.net
S/P 124

Dieffenbacher GmbH
Heilbronner Str. 20
75031 Eppingen
T +49 7262/650
www.dieffenbacher.com
S/P 31

Diono LLC
14810 Puyallup St. E, Suite 200
Sumner, WA 98390
USA
www.diono.com
S/P 185

Diono UK Ltd
35 Dale Street
Manchester, M1 2HF
UK
www.diono.com
S/P 185

Dreikant
Schwabstr. 6
99423 Weimar
T +49 3643/2 120 439
www.dreikant.net
S/P 32

E

Eis GmbH
Am Lenkwerk 3
33609 Bielefeld
T +49 800/4 450 000
www.eis.de
S/P 146, 147

ETS Extrusionstechnik Stange
Thomas-Müntzer-Str. 4
06249 Mücheln
T +49 34632/23 578
S/P 216

F

Feldschwarm Konsortium
Technische Universität Dresden
Fakultät Maschinenwesen
Institut für Naturstofftechnik
01062 Dresden
T +49 351/46 332 777
www.feldschwarm.de
S/P 40

Floyd GmbH
Frei-Otto-Str. 6
80797 München
T +49 89/997 427 330
www.floyd.one
S/P 93

Formquadrat GmbH
Brucknerstr. 3-5
A-4020 Linz
+43 732/777 244
www.formquadrat.com
S/P 133

G

Goldcard Smart Group Co. Ltd.
No. 158 Jinqiao Street
310018 Hangzhou
China
T +86 571/56 633 333
www.china-goldcard.com/en.php
S/P 33

H

Hahn Automation GmbH
Liebshausener Str. 3
55494 Rheinböllen
T +49 6764/90 220
www.smartsolutions.global
S/P 32

Hawo GmbH
Obere Au 2-4
74847 Obrigheim
T +49 6261/97 700
www.hawo.com
S/P 61

Hella Gutmann Solutions GmbH
Am Krebsbach 2
79241 Ihringen
T +49 7668/99 000
www.hella-gutmann.com
S/P 179

Howe a/s
Filosofgangen 18
DK-5000 Odense C
T +45 63/416 400
www.howe.com
S/P 85, 86

I

IADC GmbH
Siemensstr. 8
40885 Ratingen
T +49 2102/1 481
www.iadc.com.de
S/P 66

Invacare International GmbH
Benkenstr. 260
CH-4108 Witterswil
T +41 79/2147 338
www.invacare.com
S/P 51

ITKE – Universität Stuttgart
Keplerstr. 11
70174 Stuttgart
T +49 711/68 582 770
www.itke.uni-stuttgart.de
S/P 216

K

Dagmar Korintenberg & Wolf Kipper
Rötestr. 32
70197 Stuttgart
T +49 711/66 487 536
www.raumservice.de
S/P 168

Rupert Kopp Product Design
Schlesische Str. 31
10997 Berlin
T +49 30/41 722 788
www.rupert-kopp.com
S/P 194

Küschall AG
Benkenstr. 260
CH-4108 Witterswil
T +41 7879/46 035
www.kuschall.com
S/P 203

L

Landeszentrale für Politische Bildung Mecklenburg-Vorpommern
Jägerweg 2
19053 Schwerin
T +49 385/58 817 950
www.lpb-mv.de
S/P 168

Livable Cities GmbH
Hafenstr. 25
68159 Mannheim
T +49 621/15 028 570
www.citydecks.de
S/P 169

Löwenstein Medical Technology GmbH & Co. KG
Kronsaalsweg 40
22525 Hamburg
T +49 40/547 020
www.loewensteinmedical.com
S/P 57
Anne Wonsyld
S/P 57

M

Mawa Design Licht- und Wohnideen
Neu-Langerwisch 36
14552 Michendorf
T +49 33205/228 822
www.mawa-design.de
S/P 126
Aloys F. Gangkofner †
S/P 126

Metreg Technologies GmbH
Tränkeweg 9
15517 Fürstenwalde
T +49 3361/7 602 080
www.metreg-technologies.de
S/P 33

Milani Design & Consulting AG
Seestr. 95
CH-8800 Thalwil
T +41 44/9 147 474
www.milani.ch
S/P 67

N

Nimbus Group GmbH
Sieglestr. 41
70469 Stuttgart
T +49 711/6 330 140
www.nimbus-lighting.com
S/P 117

O

Ongo GmbH
Klopstockstr. 51
70193 Stuttgart
T +49 711/46 907 870
www.ongo.eu
S/P 84

Ottenwälder und Ottenwälder
Sebaldplatz 6
73525 Schwäbisch Gmünd
T +49 7171/927 230
www.ottenwaelder.de
S/P 34

P

Panik Ebner Design
Quellenstr. 7
70376 Stuttgart
T +49 711/79 481 864
www.panikebnerdesign.de
S/P 192

Panoorama Gerblinger u. Wessolowski GbR
Kochelseestr. 11
81371 München
T +49 89/18 914 643
www.panoorama.de
S/P 93, 167

Pica-Marker GmbH
Picastr. 5
91356 Kirchehrenbach
T +49 9191/3 204 030
www.pica-marker.com
S/P 35
Stephan Möck
S/P 35

R

Ranger Design
Happoldstr. 71
70469 Stuttgart
T +49 711/9 931 630
www.ranger-design.com
S/P 157

Recaro Aircraft Seating GmbH & Co. KG
Daimlerstr. 21
74523 Schwäbisch Hall
T +49 791/5 037 000
www.recaro-as.com
S/P 170

Res Anima GbR
Sonnenstr. 1
86911 Dießen a. Ammersee
T +49 8807/4 390 519
www.resanima.de
S/P 80

Robbe & Berking Silbermanufaktur seit 1874 GmbH & Co. KG
Zur Bleiche 47
24941 Flensburg
T +49 461/903 060
www.robbeberking.com
S/P 108

Rökona Textilwerk GmbH & Co KG
Schaffhausenstr. 101
72072 Tübingen
T +49 7071/1 530
www.roekona.de
S/P 211

Dr. Karl-Heinz Rueß
Östliche Ringstraße 34
73033 Göppingen
S/P 157

S

Georg Schlegel GmbH & Co. KG
Kapellenweg 4
88525 Dürmentingen
T +49 7371/5 020
www.schlegel.biz
S/P 34

Richard Schmied GmbH
Elchinger Str. 14
73432 Aalen
T +49 7367/4 206
www.richardschmied.com
S/P 82

Valentin Schmied
Ebnater Hauptstr. 21
73432 Aalen
T +49 163/7 029 727
www.valentinschmied.com
S/P 82

**Serien.Lighting –
Serien Raumleuchten GmbH**
Hainhäuser Str. 3-7
63110 Rodgau
T +49 6106/69 090
www.serien.com
S/P 125

SKA Sitze GmbH
Am Oberwald 7
76744 Wörth am Rhein
T +49 7271/93 310
www.ska.de
S/P 192

**Stadt Göppingen
Archiv und Museen**
Schlossstraße 14
73033 Göppingen
www.goeppingen.de
S/P 157

**StadtPalais Stuttgart –
Museum für Stuttgart**
Konrad-Adenauer-Str. 2
70173 Stuttgart
T +49 711/21 625 800
www.stadtpalais-stuttgart.de
S/P 166

Steng Licht GmbH
Rudolf-Diesel-Str. 35
71394 Kernen
T +49 7151/903 280
www.steng.de
S/P 124

Stephan Kommunikationsdesign
Werderstr. 43
76137 Karlsruhe
T +49 721 9093 009
www.stephan-design.com
S/P 57

Störiko Product Design GmbH
Godeffroystr. 40
22587 Hamburg
T +49 172/2 115 835
www.stoeriko.net
S/P 85, 86

Supernova Design GmbH & Co. KG
Industriestr. 26
79194 Gundelfingen
T +49 761/6 006 290
www.supernova-lights.com
S/P 139

Swarovski Optik KG
Daniel-Swarovski-Straße 70
A-6067 Absam
T +43 5223/5 110
www.swarovskioptik.com
S/P 133

Systemceram GmbH & Co. KG
Berggarten 1
56427 Siershahn
T +49 2623/60 010
www.systemceram.de
S/P 66

T

Technisches Design TU Dresden
August-Bebel-Str. 20
01219 Dresden
T +49 351/46 335 750
www.tu-dresden.de/ing/
maschinenwesen/imm/td
S/P 40

U

Uhrenfabrik Junghans GmbH & Co. KG
Geißhaldenstr. 49
78713 Schramberg
T +49 7422/180
www.junghans.de
S/P 99

UP Designstudio GmbH & Co. KG
Dornierstr. 17
70469 Stuttgart
T +49 711/3 265 460
www.updesignstudio.com
S/P 51, 84, 203

V

V&B Fliesen GmbH
Rotensteiner Weg
66663 Merzig
T +49 6864/813 296
www.pro.villeroy-boch.com
S/P 217
Axel Buether, Prof. Dr.
S/P 217

**Visuell Studio für
Kommunikation GmbH**
Tübingerstr. 97a
70178 Stuttgart
T +49 711/648 680
www.visuell.de
S/P 166

V-Zug AG
Industriestr. 66
CH-6305 Zug
T +41 58/7 676 767
www.vzug.com
S/P 67

V-Zug Europe BV
Evolis 102
BE-8530 Harelbeke
www.vzug.com
S/P 67

W

Walkolution GmbH
Gewerbestr. 1
97355 Wiesenbronn
T +49 322/21 853 977
www.walkolution.com
S/P 81

**Wasserzweckverband Rottenburger
Gruppe**
Am Wasserwerk 1
84056 Rottenburg a. d. Laaber
T +49 8781/94 130
www.rottenburger-gruppe.de
S/P 167

Wd3 GmbH
Seidenstr. 57
70174 Stuttgart
T +49 711/28 497 720
www.wd3.design
S/P 80

Karl Westermann GmbH & Co.KG
Albstr. 1
73770 Denkendorf
T + 49 711/9 344 600
www.westermann.com
S/P 80

White ID GmbH & Co. KG
Nicolaus-Otto-Str. 8
73614 Schorndorf
T +49 7181/991 980
www.white-id.com
S/P 185

Wiha Werkzeuge GmbH
Obertalstr. 3-7
78136 Schonach
T +49 7722/9 590
www.wiha.com
S/P 30

Winkelbauer-Design
Myliusstr. 3
71638 Ludwigsburg
T +49 7141/903 222
www.winkelbauer-design.de
S/P 35

NAMENSREGISTER / INDEX OF NAMES

A

AMF – Andreas Maier GmbH & Co. KG
S/P 21

B

b+a Vertriebs GmbH
S/P 148
Bene GmbH
S/P 83
bKing Design
S/P 107
Botta Design
S/P 106
Brennenstuhl, Dietrich
S/P 118
Buether, Prof. Dr. Axel
S/P 217

C

Code2Design
S/P 33

D

Daytona Corporation
S/P 193
Daytona Europe
S/P 193
Defortec GmbH
S/P 31, 179
Designstudio Speziell
S/P 124
Dieffenbacher GmbH
S/P 31
Diono LLC
S/P 185
Diono UK Ltd
S/P 185
Dreikant
S/P 32

E

Eis GmbH
S/P 146, 147
ETS Extrusionstechnik Stange
S/P 216

F

Farina, Domenico
S/P 22
Feldschwarm Konsortium
S/P 40
Floyd GmbH
S/P 93
Formquadrat GmbH
S/P 133

G

Gerblinger, Julian
S/P 94
Goldcard Smart Group Co. Ltd.
S/P 33

H

Hahn Automation GmbH
S/P 32
Hawo GmbH
S/P 61
Hella Gutmann Solutions GmbH
S/P 179
Hess, Andreas
S/P 186
Horner, Christian
S/P 83
Howe a/s
S/P 85, 86
Huth, Bernd
S/P 193

I

IADC GmbH
S/P 66
Invacare International GmbH
S/P 51
ITKE – Universität Stuttgart
S/P 216

K

King, Bernadett
S/P 107
Kipper, Wolf
S/P 168
Klobertanz, Ilja
S/P 180
Rupert Kopp Product Design
S/P 194
Korintenberg, Dagmar
S/P 168
Krzywinski, Jens
S/P 42
Küschall AG
S/P 203

L

Landeszentrale für Politische Bildung Mecklenburg-Vorpommern
S/P 168
Lippert, Stefan
S/P 52, 204
Livable Cities GmbH
S/P 169
Löwenstein Medical Technology GmbH & Co. KG
S/P 57

M

Mawa Design GmbH
S/P 126
Metreg Technologies GmbH
S/P 33
Milani Design & Consulting AG
S/P 67
Möck, Stephan
S/P 35

N

Nimbus Group GmbH
S/P 117

O

Ongo GmbH
S/P 84
Ottenwälder und Ottenwälder
S/P 34

P

Panik Ebner Design
S/P 192
Panoorama
S/P 93, 167
Pica-Marker GmbH
S/P 35

R

Ranger Design
S/P 157
Ranger, Kurt
S/P 158

Recaro Aircraft Seating GmbH & Co. KG
S/P 170
Res Anima GbR
S/P 80
Robbe & Berking Silbermanufaktur seit 1874 GmbH & Co. KG
S/P 108
Rökona Textilwerk GmbH & Co KG
S/P 211
Rueß, Dr. Karl-Heinz
S/P 157

S

Schäfer, Katharina
S/P 212
Georg Schlegel GmbH & Co. KG
S/P 34
Richard Schmied GmbH
S/P 82
Schmied, Valentin
S/P 82
Serien.Lighting – Serien Raumleuchten GmbH
S/P 125
SKA Sitze GmbH
S/P 192
Stadt Göppingen
S/P 157
StadtPalais Stuttgart – Museum für Stuttgart
S/P 166
Steng Licht GmbH
S/P 124
Stephan Kommunikationsdesign
S/P 57
Störiko Product Design GmbH
S/P 85, 86
Stotz, Matthias
S/P 100
Supernova Design GmbH & Co. KG
S/P 139
Swarovski Optik KG
S/P 133
Systemceram GmbH & Co. KG
S/P 66

T

Tams, Nikolaus
S/P 193
Technisches Design TU Dresden
S/P 40

U

Uhrenfabrik Junghans GmbH & Co. KG
S/P 99
UP Designstudio GmbH & Co. KG
S/P 51, 84, 203

V

V&B Fliesen GmbH
S/P 217
Visuell Studio für Kommunikation GmbH
S/P 166
V-Zug AG
S/P 67
V-Zug Europe BV
S/P 67

W

Wallmeyer, Marcus
S/P 140
Walkolution GmbH
S/P 81
Wasserzweckverband Rottenburger Gruppe
S/P 167
wd3 GmbH
S/P 80
Karl Westermann GmbH & Co.KG
S/P 80
White ID GmbH & Co. KG
S/P 185

Wiha Werkzeuge GmbH
S/P 30
Winkelbauer-Design
S/P 35
Wonsyld, Anne
S/P 57

Z

Zeppetzauer, Mario
S/P 134

LET'S THANK ...

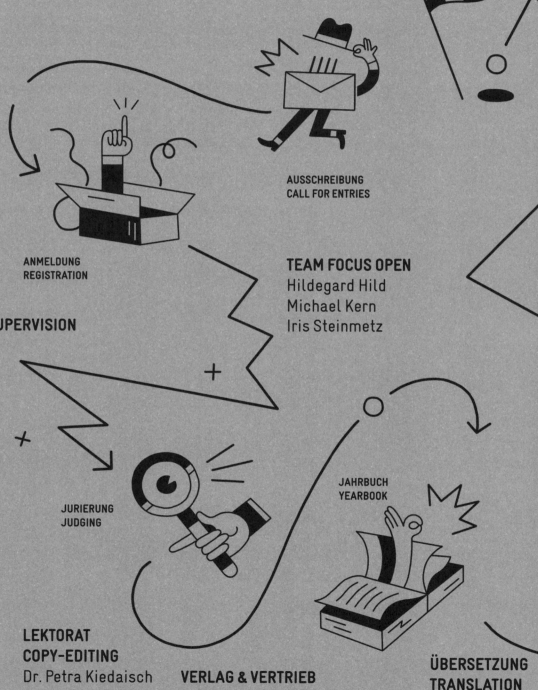

GRAFIKDESIGN
GRAPHIC DESIGN
stapelberg&fritz gmbh
Julian Hölzer
Daniel Fritz

TEXT & REDAKTION
TEXT & EDITORIAL SUPERVISION
Armin Scharf

JURY
Dr. Sybs Bauer
Sven von Boetticher
Susanne Ewert
Tina Kammer
Gerrit Terstiege
Tilo Wüsthoff

LEKTORAT
COPY-EDITING
Dr. Petra Kiedaisch
Gabriele Betz
Armin Scharf

ANMELDUNG
REGISTRATION

AUSSCHREIBUNG
CALL FOR ENTRIES

TEAM FOCUS OPEN
Hildegard Hild
Michael Kern
Iris Steinmetz

JURIERUNG
JUDGING

JAHRBUCH
YEARBOOK

VERLAG & VERTRIEB
PUBLISHING & DISTRIBUTION
avedition
Dr. Petra Kiedaisch

ÜBERSETZUNG
TRANSLATION
Alison Du Bovis

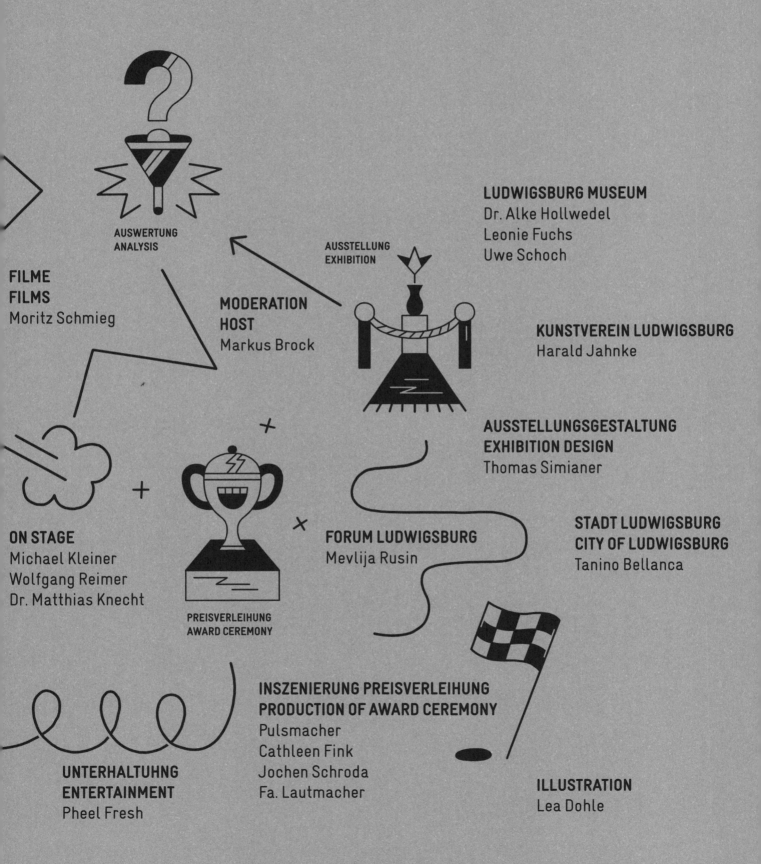

DESIGN IM DIALOG

Beratung, Fortbildung, Information und Präsentationen – das Design Center Baden-Württemberg ist eine nicht-kommerzielle Plattform für Design-Profis, Einsteiger und Unternehmer zugleich

DESIGN LESE
Vorträge, Medienpräsentationen und Diskussionsrunden zu aktuellen Themenbereichen aus Industrie, Design, Technik, Forschung und Wirtschaft.

DESIGN LESE LECTURES
Lectures, media presentations and panel discussions on up-to-the-minute topics from industry, design, technology, research and business.

EINSICHTEN
Austauschplattform für Industrie, Designwirtschaft, Forschung und Ausbildung. Unternehmen, Designagenturen und auch Design-Ausbildungsstätten erhalten die Möglichkeit, sich im Haus der Wirtschaft in Stuttgart detailliert zu präsentieren.

EINSICHTEN PRESENTATION PLATFORM
A platform for industry, the design sector, research and education where companies, design agencies and design schools are given the opportunity to stage detailed presentations at the Haus der Wirtschaft in Stuttgart.

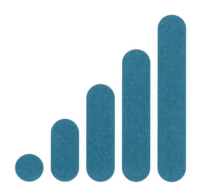

DESIGN1ST BERATUNG
Im Rahmen unserer kostenfreien Design1st Beratung erhalten Unternehmer*innen Auskunft zu allen Fragen rund um Designleistungen und zu direkten Kooperationsmöglichkeiten mit der Designwirtschaft.

DESIGN1ST ADVISORY SERVICE
Our free Design1st advisory service provides entrepreneurs with information about anything to do with design services and advises them on the possibilities for direct cooperation with the design sector.

FIT FOR MARKET
Der richtige Schutz innovativer Produkte, die Anmeldung von Marken, die Honorierung kreativer Leistung oder die Vertragsgestaltung mit Designer*innen sind Themenfelder dieser Veranstaltungsreihe.

FIT FOR MAKET
This series of events covers topics like the right protection for innovative products, registering trademarks, appropriate payment for creative services and contractual arrangements with designers.

DESIGN IN DIALOGUE

Advice, training, information and presentations – the Design Center Baden-Württemberg is a non-commercial platform aimed not just at design professionals but at newcomers and entrepreneurs too.

DESIGN CENTER ROADSHOW
Veranstaltungen mit und bei unterschiedlichsten externen Kooperationspartnern, als Foren des Austauschs zwischen Industrie und Designwirtschaft.

DESIGN CENTER ROADSHOW
Events hosted by a wide range of external cooperation partners as forums where industry and the design sector can swap ideas and views.

DESIGN BIBLIOTHEK
Präsenzbibliothek für Designprofis und Designinteressierte, mit Online-Katalog und einem spezialisierten Publikationsbestand von rund 10.000 Büchern rund um das Thema Gestaltung.

DESIGN LIBRARY
A bricks-and-mortar library for design professionals and anyone interested in design, with an online catalogue and a specialised collection of around 10,000 publications on all aspects of design.

ENTDECKT
Die Präsentationsplattform für den Designnachwuchs! Vielversprechende Designtalente erhalten die Möglichkeit, sich samt ihrer aktuellen Projekte im Design Center der breiten Öffentlichkeit zu präsentieren.

ENTDECKT SHOWCASE
A presentation platform for up-and-coming designers that gives promising and talented newcomers the chance to introduce themselves and their latest projects to a broad public at the Design Center.

KONGRESSE & WORKSHOPS
Veranstaltungen zur Vermittlung von Know-how aus den unterschiedlichsten designrelevanten Disziplinen und Forschungsbereichen, aber auch aus dem weiten Feld des Marketings.

CONGRESSES & WORKSHOPS
Events that share know-how from all sorts of design-relevant disciplines and research areas, as well as from the broad field of marketing.

IMPRESSUM / PUBLISHING DETAILS

HERAUSGEBER / PUBLISHER
Design Center Baden-Württemberg
Regierungspräsidium Stuttgart
Willi-Bleicher-Straße 19
70174 Stuttgart
T +49 711 123 26 84
design@rps.bwl.de
www.design-center.de

**TEXT UND REDAKTION /
TEXT AND EDITORIAL SUPERVISION**
Armin Scharf
Tübingen
www.bueroscharf.de

LEKTORAT / COPY-EDITING
Petra Kiedaisch
Armin Scharf
Gabriele Betz
Tübingen
www.gabriele-betz.de

ÜBERSETZUNG / TRANSLATION
Alison Du Bovis
Jork
www.dubovis.de

GRAFIKDESIGN / GRAPHIC DESIGN
stapelberg&fritz GmbH
Julian Hölzer
Daniel Fritz
Stuttgart
www.stapelbergundfritz.com

ILLUSTRATIONEN / ILLUSTRATIONS
Lea Dohle Illustration Stuttgart
www.leadohle.de
Instagram @leadohle

LITHOGRAFIE / LITHOGRAPHY
Corinna Rieber Prepress
www.rieber-prepress.de

DRUCK / PRINTING
Offizin Scheufele GmbH + Co. KG
Stuttgart
www.scheufele.de

PAPIER / PAPER
Juwel Offset,
PEFC-zertifiziert /
PEFC certified

**VERLAG UND VERTRIEB /
PUBLISHING AND DISTRIBUTION**
av edition GmbH
Senefelderstraße 109
70176 Stuttgart
T +49 711 / 2202279-0
kontakt@avedition.de
www.avedition.de

© 2021
av edition GmbH,
Design Center Baden-Württemberg
und die Autoren / and the authors

Alle Rechte vorbehalten. /
All rights reserved.

ISBN 978-3-89986-354-3
Printed in Germany

Die Publikation erscheint
anlässlich der Ausstellung
»Focus Open 2021 –
Internationaler Designpreis
Baden-Württemberg
und Mia Seeger Preis 2021«

09. Oktober
bis 21. November 2021

This catalogue is published to
accompany the exhibition
»Focus Open 2021 –
Baden-Württemberg International
Design Award and
Mia Seeger Prize 2021«

9 October
to 21 November 2021

VERANSTALTER / ORGANISER
Design Center Baden-Württemberg
Regierungspräsidium Stuttgart
Willi-Bleicher-Straße 19
70174 Stuttgart
T +49 711 123 26 84

**VERANTWORTUNG UND KONZEPTION /
RESPONSIBILITY AND CONCEPT**
Christiane Nicolaus

**PROJEKTLEITUNG /
PROJECT MANAGER**
Hildegard Hild

ORGANISATION / ADMINISTRATION
Michael Kern

**AUSSTELLUNGSGESTALTUNG /
EXHIBITION DESIGN**
Thomas Simianer

**INSZENIERUNG PREISVERLEIHUNG /
PRODUCTION OF AWARD CEREMONY**
pulsmacher
Ludwigsburg
www.pulsmacher.de